THE BEDFORD SERIES IN HISTORY AND CULTURE

Jackie Robinson and Race in America

A Brief History with Documents

Related Titles in
THE BEDFORD SERIES IN HISTORY AND CULTURE
Advisory Editors: Lynn Hunt, *University of California, Los Angeles*
David W. Blight, *Yale University*
Bonnie G. Smith, *Rutgers University*
Natalie Zemon Davis, *University of Toronto*

THE BEDFORD SERIES IN HISTORY AND CULTURE

Jackie Robinson and Race in America

A Brief History with Documents

Thomas W. Zeiler

University of Colorado Boulder

BEDFORD / ST. MARTIN'S   Boston ◆ New York

For Bedford/St. Martin's

Publisher for History: Mary V. Dougherty
Senior Executive Editor for History: William J. Lombardo
Director of Development for History: Jane Knetzger
Senior Editor: Heidi L. Hood
Executive Editor: Elizabeth M. Welch
Publishing Services Manager: Andrea Cava
Production Supervisor: Victoria Anzalone
Executive Marketing Manager: Sandra McGuire
Editorial Assistant: Laura Kintz
Project Management: Books By Design, Inc.
Text Design: Claire Seng-Niemoeller
Cover Design: Marine Miller
Cover Photo: National Baseball Hall of Fame Library, Cooperstown, N.Y.
Composition: Achorn International, Inc.
Printing and Binding: RR Donnelley and Sons

President, Bedford/St. Martin's: Denise B. Wydra
Director of Marketing: Karen R. Soeltz
Production Director: Susan W. Brown
Director of Rights and Permissions: Hilary Newman

For information, write: Bedford / St. Martin's, 75 Arlington Street, Boston, MA 02116 (617-399-4000)

ISBN 978-1-4576-1788-1

Acknowledgments

Acknowledgments and copyrights are continued at the back of the book on page 154, which constitutes an extension of the copyright page. It is a violation of the law to reproduce these selections by any means whatsoever without the written permission of the copyright holder.

About the cover: Jackie Robinson entered Ebbets Field on April 10, 1947, as a Montreal Royal, and he left as a member of the Brooklyn Dodgers.

Foreword

The Bedford Series in History and Culture is designed so that readers can study the past as historians do.

The historian's first task is finding the evidence. Documents, letters, memoirs, interviews, pictures, movies, novels, or poems can provide facts and clues. Then the historian questions and compares the sources. There is more to do than in a courtroom, for hearsay evidence is welcome, and the historian is usually looking for answers beyond act and motive. Different views of an event may be as important as a single verdict. How a story is told may yield as much information as what it says.

Along the way the historian seeks help from other historians and perhaps from specialists in other disciplines. Finally, it is time to write, to decide on an interpretation and how to arrange the evidence for readers.

Each book in this series contains an important historical document or group of documents, each document a witness from the past and open to interpretation in different ways. The documents are combined with some element of historical narrative — an introduction or a biographical essay, for example — that provides students with an analysis of the primary source material and important background information about the world in which it was produced.

Each book in the series focuses on a specific topic within a specific historical period. Each provides a basis for lively thought and discussion about several aspects of the topic and the historian's role. Each is short enough (and inexpensive enough) to be a reasonable one-week assignment in a college course. Whether as classroom or personal reading, each book in the series provides firsthand experience of the challenge — and fun — of discovering, recreating, and interpreting the past.

Lynn Hunt
David W. Blight
Bonnie G. Smith
Natalie Zemon Davis

Preface

"Whoever wants to know the heart and mind of America had better learn baseball," wrote the French-born scholar Jacques Barzun in 1954. Baseball has often reflected American life and society, and never more so than in the mid-twentieth century, when it rightfully was named the national pastime. One figure stands out among the tens of thousands of people involved in the professional sport over the past three centuries, however: Jack Roosevelt "Jackie" Robinson (1919–1972).

Robinson emerged from a humble background to engage the nation in extraordinary circumstances. He was a black man in a white man's country who participated in twentieth-century America's major social movement: the struggle for civil rights. By helping to break the color barrier in America's premier sport and one of the country's most visible laboratories for social experimentation, Jackie Robinson the ballplayer created even bigger victories off the field than on it.

His famous deed, in the early afternoon of April 15, 1947, was quite simple in terms of baseball accomplishments, but it was monumental in the life of the nation. That day, he appeared in the uniform of the Brooklyn Dodgers of the National League, at Ebbets Field, the Dodgers' ballpark, and played first base. When he ran out of the dugout to take the field in the first inning, his steps erased a color line that had banned blacks from playing America's national pastime at the highest professional level for more than a half-century. Robinson's major league debut dealt a blow to the Jim Crow segregation that had plagued the United States since the Civil War, and it set the nation on the road to racial integration that culminated nearly two decades later in the Civil Rights Act of 1964 and the Voting Rights Act of 1965. Explaining how Robinson got to that point, why the nation reached this crossroads, and the response from many quarters of American life is the purpose of this book.

The scholarship on Robinson and on baseball is vast, but I sensed history instructors' need for a short, document-based book that would set Robinson's major league debut in the proper historical context. *Jackie*

Robinson and Race in America: A Brief History with Documents takes our eyes off the ball to examine how the nation's most popular sport reflected the broader social and cultural arenas that surrounded it at a pivotal moment in American history. It opens with an introduction that traces the history of Robinson's feat and its meaning and legacy. While the introduction weaves Robinson's entire life story into the larger narrative of U.S. race relations, the primary-source documents, the core of the book, focus on the course of events that led to his major league debut, its impact on baseball and the greater society, and Robinson's—and baseball's—place in the movement toward racial integration.

Selectivity is necessary to manage the tremendous volume of primary-source materials about Robinson while also providing the views of the group most directly affected by his entry into professional white baseball: African Americans. Thus this volume includes documents from a range of perspectives: sports and mainstream white commentators, academics, participants in baseball, and especially the black press and community. Many of the African American newspapers represented here no longer exist, and their inclusion allows students to appreciate the vital role that black voices played in Robinson's historic achievement. We hear from Robinson himself as well, both during his playing career, when he followed Dodgers general manager Branch Rickey's admonition to "turn the other cheek" in pursuit of long-term goals, and after, when he no longer felt constrained about speaking out against racism.

To facilitate students' analysis of the sources, each document opens with a headnote that provides historical context. Explanatory footnotes appear where useful to clarify the events described. At the end of the volume, students and instructors will find a chronology that sets Robinson's life and career in the larger context of U.S. race relations, a list of questions suitable for discussion or for writing assignments, and a selected bibliography with suggestions for further reading.

ACKNOWLEDGMENTS

A number of people helped me write this book. The following historians contributed generously of their time and knowledge to review early drafts, and I thank them for their helpful critiques: Andy Deroche, Front Range Community College; Jelani Favors, Morgan State University; Marc Gallicchio, Villanova University; Aram Goudsouzian, University of Memphis; Eric Hall, Georgia Southern University; Richard Kimball, Brigham Young University; Charles Ross, University of Mississippi; Rob Ruck, University of Pittsburgh; the late Jules Tygiel, San Francisco State University; and John R. M. Wilson, Vanguard University.

I thank David Blight, advisory editor for the Bedford Series in History and Culture, for supporting this volume. I also thank Mary V. Dougherty, publisher for history; William J. Lombardo, senior executive editor for history; Heidi L. Hood, senior editor; Laura Kintz, editorial assistant; Andrea Cava, publishing services manager; Nancy Benjamin, project manager; Barbara Jatkola, copy editor; and Elizabeth M. Welch, executive editor. However, I need to single out a few from this list. Bill Lombardo urged me to write this volume, and I thank him for his encouragement. Laura Kintz, with good cheer, helped the entire process along, especially the procurement of copyright permissions, an onerous task. The contributions of Nancy Benjamin and Barbara Jatkola were simply sensational. But above all, Beth Welch was an extraordinary source of support from start to finish. Her enthusiasm for the project, her clear explanations of reviewers' reports, her masterful editing, and her wise guidance throughout made this a much better book than I could have produced on my own. I will even cut Beth some slack for being a Red Sox fan!

I especially thank Rachel Robinson, Jackie Robinson's wife, and her assistant at the Jackie Robinson Foundation, Mireille Stephen, for so generously granting permission to reproduce several documents in this book.

On a personal note, I would like to thank family and friends, as well as the many students over the years who have taken my course America through Baseball and have added to my baseball knowledge and appreciation for Robinson. One of my graduate students, Rob Morrison, worked tirelessly to collect documents and secure copyright permissions; he deserves much credit for his help. Marc Jackson, foreign service officer extraordinaire and a wonderful friend, read the manuscript with an eye toward improving the writing, and I thank him for the effort. My father instilled in me a deep love of baseball and sports, even though we are more often than not frustrated Braves fans. As usual, I thank Rocio, Jackson, and Ella for being just who they are, my favorite people in the world. And who knows: One day, our Colorado Rockies might win it all.

Thomas W. Zeiler

Contents

PART ONE

Introduction: America's Great Experiment of Baseball Integration

*It's true that I've been the laboratory specimen in a great change in orga-
nized baseball.* —Jackie Robinson, July 1949

In the rotunda of Citi Field, home of the New York Mets baseball club, stands a big blue number 42. Surrounding plaques highlight the date April 15, designated by Major League Baseball as a day of commemoration. On that date in 1947, Jackie Robinson—number 42—changed history. His is the sole number displayed in every big league ballpark in the United States. It was the first to be retired, in 1997, by every team in any major American sport.

Jackie Robinson's play at the Brooklyn Dodgers' ballpark, Ebbets Field, on the afternoon of April 15, 1947, was minor in terms of baseball accomplishments. Indeed, though the Dodgers won, Robinson did not record a hit. In the life of the nation, however, it was monumental. Dubbed the national pastime, baseball at the time enjoyed more acclaim than American football does today. Through radio and newspapers, the masses followed games day by day. Unlike the Internet of today, with its myriad outlets that disperse news widely and constantly, radio and newspapers in the 1940s were the main sources of reportage nationwide, running stories that unified the entire American public around the sport. In an era when Americans *lived* baseball, Jackie Robinson was the story of the time.

Thus April 15, 1947, is a date—like April 12, 1861, when the Battle of Fort Sumter ignited the U.S. Civil War, or December 7, 1941, when the Japanese attack on Pearl Harbor sparked the U.S. entry into World War II—that changed the United States irrevocably. When Robinson ran out of the dugout to take the field in the first inning that day, his steps erased a half-century-old color line that had prevented blacks from playing America's national pastime at the highest professional level. One of Robinson's biographers, Jules Tygiel, labeled it "baseball's great experiment."[1] Professional baseball had become the laboratory to test American principles of equality and fairness.

The contested terrain of race relations that followed Robinson's achievement—in sports, politics, and society as a whole—attests to the sober reality of its impact. His story, like the wider history of racial integration in America, circled back on itself: Progress hit a wall of resistance shaped by deep-seated attitudes of racism and race consciousness, and then the campaign for equal rights began anew. Robinson's iconic status rests on his feat's symbolic meaning. For some, his accomplishment is the stuff of legend, but for others it is a sad reminder of the cycles of history. Symbolism meets historical reality in at least one critical respect, however: Robinson unlocked possibilities for resolving America's distinctive problem of race.

ROBINSON'S EARLY YEARS

Jackie Robinson was born on January 31, 1919, in Cairo, Georgia. He entered a world familiar to many African Americans at the time, one characterized by rural poverty, prejudice and segregation, migration from the South, and strong mothers heading single-parent families. The Robinsons moved to Pasadena, California, near Los Angeles, in 1923, when Jackie was four years old. There they lived among an interracial mix of blacks, Asians, Mexicans, and whites. Following the example of his older brother Mack, who later won a silver medal at the Berlin Olympics in 1936, Jackie excelled in sports early on. Because of his athletic ability, he more than stood his ground against more affluent white youths, earning a reputation among whites for being "uppity." Once when he was a teenager, during a verbal dispute with police over a traffic incident, he lashed out in response to the officers' racial epithets.

This was a justified, but imprudent, reaction in America at that time. To be sure, the Ku Klux Klan had declined in numbers from its heyday the decade before, and civil rights organizations such as the National

Association for the Advancement of Colored People (NAACP) and spokesmen such as Marcus Garvey and W. E. B. Du Bois spurred African Americans' pursuit of racial justice. In addition, the Harlem Renaissance of the 1920s had boosted the creative side of the black experience; writers, musicians, and actors made African American culture a point of pride in the black community. Nonetheless, African Americans remained oppressed by the dominant white society.

During the cataclysm of the Great Depression, from 1929 to 1941, most stable black businesses folded. Rendered defenseless by the economic calamity, average white people could count on New Deal federal aid to farmers, workers, and the unemployed, but southern legislators excluded African Americans from many key relief programs, including Social Security, designed to provide a modest income to relieve the poverty of elderly people. After years of decline, the lynching of blacks skyrocketed during the Depression. In Alabama, the black "Scottsboro Boys" faced the death penalty in 1931 for a murder they did not commit, and up north a 1935 riot in Harlem, where the artistic renaissance had once flourished, dramatized African Americans' despair and frustration.

Robinson's success in sports at John Muir Technical High School, Pasadena Junior College, and the University of California, Los Angeles (UCLA), shielded him somewhat from such hostile forms of discrimination. By the end of his first year at UCLA, the nation recognized him as the "Jim Thorpe of his race," a reference to the early-twentieth-century Native American Olympian and multisport athlete known as the most versatile sports figure in history. Robinson actually outshined Thorpe. Coaches called him the best basketball player in the country and one of the finest running backs in collegiate football. Robinson was the national junior college champion in the broad jump, won the Pacific Coast Intercollegiate Golf Championship, won the junior boys singles championship in the Pacific Coast Negro Tennis Tournament, and captured swimming titles at UCLA. Baseball, surprisingly enough, was his weakest sport, though scouts asserted that if the major leagues had allowed blacks, he would have been a top prospect for many teams.[2]

Convinced that a college degree would not help a black man get a job during the Great Depression, Robinson dropped out of UCLA in early 1941. He became assistant athletic director of the local branch of the National Youth Administration, but soon this New Deal agency shut down, and he moved to Hawaii to play semiprofessional football for the racially integrated Honolulu Bears in the fall of 1941. That December, when the team moved to Los Angeles to join the Pacific Coast Football League, Robinson returned to California to try out as a running back.

With the United States' entry into World War II that same month, however, the twenty-two-year-old Robinson was soon drafted into military service.

BASEBALL, THE NATIONAL PASTIME

That Robinson would become drawn to professional baseball was not surprising, owing to its stature in American sports and society. Once rules were set in place in the 1840s by Alexander Cartwright of the New York Knickerbockers, amateur baseball teams represented by trades and businesses dominated the game until 1869, when the Cincinnati Red Stockings became the first play-for-pay professional team. In the ensuing decades, the regulations and financial structure of the National League (established in 1876) and the American League (founded in 1901), and their junior and training teams in the minor leagues, became known as "organized baseball." Until 1953, when the Boston Braves moved to Milwaukee, the major leagues consisted of the same sixteen teams, divided evenly into the National and American leagues and located in the Northeast and Midwest. An annual World Series pitted the champions, or pennant winners, of the two leagues against each other.

Between 1890 and 1950, baseball was the most popular sport in America, even as football and basketball began to encroach on its cultural monopoly. By the turn of the century, modern playing grounds held thousands of spectators and transformed urban areas. Journalists covered the games to satisfy the growing number of "fanatics" (shortened to "fans"), devising special "box scores" to summarize the results and save space in newspapers (Document 13). Ty Cobb, Christy Mathewson, Walter Johnson, and Honus Wagner became household names. A "dead-ball" era, in which pitching dominated hitting from 1900 through World War I due to a soft, unraveling ball and a low-scoring strategy of carefully advancing runners by stolen bases and sacrifice bunts and singles, gave way to the "age of [Babe] Ruth" and the home run kings of subsequent decades. Americans marveled at the play on the field and idolized the players and teams off it.

All was not well in the baseball world, however. Players vied with owners over rising profits, salaries, and restrictions on their ability to change teams (and cities) under the "reserve clause."[3] Labor strife turned into crisis when eight of the Chicago White Sox, the prohibitive favorite in the 1919 World Series, purposely lost the championship. They did so to protest their treatment by their miserly owner, Charles

Comiskey, but the scandal caused an uproar among the American public. In response, a new commissioner's office—ruled with an iron fist by Kenesaw Mountain Landis from 1920 to 1944—aimed to restore confidence in America's pastime by issuing lifetime bans on playing or attending games in the major leagues to all eight players. The austere Landis got credit for saving the game.

Thus baseball continued to flourish, even beyond America's shores. It was the subject of world tours and exhibitions. Immigrants learned to play the game, or become expert observers of it, as a means to enter American society. Minority communities embraced the sport as well. But organized baseball, like America itself, held the door only partially open to these newcomers.

JIM CROW ON THE BASEBALL DIAMOND

White America deemed the professional game off-limits to African Americans, just as the U.S. Supreme Court laid down the "separate but equal" principle that legalized racial segregation throughout the nation under its 1896 *Plessy v. Ferguson* decision. In the decades following the Civil War and Reconstruction, restrictive laws that segregated blacks, called Jim Crow laws, became common throughout the South. *Plessy v. Ferguson* gave federal endorsement to racial segregation, but white players and executives had already drawn the color line in baseball nearly a decade earlier, around 1887–1888, by banning black players. In 1888, Moses Fleetwood Walker, the first black major leaguer, became the last African American to play in the major leagues. According to the first historian of black baseball, Robert Peterson, "The truth was plain for all who wished to see it: Jim Crow was warming up."[4]

African Americans were not the only minorities to face discrimination in baseball. Jewish players were shunned or taunted, forced to Anglicize their names (from Cohen to Connor, for instance), and stereotyped as money-hungry contract negotiators.[5] Supposedly hotheaded Latinos were deemed too emotional for the majors, and Latin American players were treated as people of color.[6] Whites referred to Native American players as "Chief" and considered them prone to alcoholism and, consequently, employment risks. There is evidence that Cleveland residents in the late 1890s intended to honor the Penobscot player Louis Sockalexis of the Cleveland Spiders by renaming the team "Indians," but the new name was seen as another display of ethnic and racial stereotyping.[7]

African Americans occupied the bottom rung of the Jim Crow ladder, however. They were specific targets of segregation. Baseball accepted white European immigrants as players and fans, thus gaining them acceptance as Americans. Yet black players, fans, and owners, American citizens themselves, were denied the right to participate in the national pastime because of their color. Their predicament was part of African Americans' larger struggle against racism, and as in other areas of society, they could apply pressure against discrimination only where and in ways that it was safe to do so. Black players, therefore, had two options for playing professional baseball. First, they could try to "pass" as Native Americans or "Cubans," a choice that was not only demeaning but rarely successful.[8] Pitcher Jimmy Claxton, for example, played in the Pacific Coast League for a week in 1916 but was dismissed immediately after being identified as black. Second, they could seek employment in all-black leagues or abroad.

African American teams had existed since the early days of Reconstruction. Segregated baseball showed the great injustice of Jim Crow, yet the Negro Leagues (the generic name for the organized black major leagues from 1920 through the 1940s) also provided opportunities for black players, executives, and towns to thrive in an unequal United States. Among the first national black institutions to emerge after Reconstruction, the Negro Leagues brought cohesion to communities at the local and national levels and gave African Americans a stage on which to perform with grace, competence, and dignity.

The Negro Leagues drew on a long history of black baseball. From 1867, when Philadelphia and New York squads staged a "Colored Championship," to 1885, the year the Cuban Giants became the first black professional team, in Babylon, New York, African Americans participated in all aspects of baseball. The ensuing decades witnessed black circuits, most of which struggled financially. Savvy businessmen, however, such as Andrew "Rube" Foster in New York and Frank Leland in Chicago, organized lucrative teams. Capitalizing on the Great Migration, in which hundreds of thousands of blacks left the South for the Northeast and Midwest during World War I, and recognizing that African Americans, like whites, represented a growing fan base for the national pastime, Foster and others formed the Negro National League in 1920, with teams in Chicago, Dayton (Ohio), Saint Louis, Kansas City (Missouri), Indianapolis, and Detroit. The founding of the Negro National League touched off an era of professional baseball spectacular by any standard.

Over the next three decades, some eight Negro Leagues emerged under various owners, all of them with ties to black business or political communities and some with connections to the criminal world. Parades heralded the beginning of the season, communities rallied around their teams, and advertisements for games were to be found in every bar, store, and barbershop. Politicians of all colors attended opening day; in New York City, it was imperative during elections for mayoral candidates to show up at games. The Negro Leagues also provided opportunities for civic engagement, serving, for example, as a forum for the civil rights movement.

Such was the case for Effa Manley, the mixed-race co-owner (with her husband, Abe) of the Newark Eagles and one of the few female owners in baseball (Document 20). In 1934, as treasurer of the local NAACP branch, Manley arranged a successful boycott of New York City department stores that refused to hire blacks. Five years later, she held what she dubbed "Anti-Lynching Day" at the Eagles' Ruppert Stadium. At a time when southern legislators held up antilynching bills in Congress and President Franklin D. Roosevelt shied away from them out of a fear of losing votes in the region, Manley's campaign helped build support for decisive political action to outlaw the crime.

Meanwhile, black baseball flourished. Racketeer and bootlegger Gus Greenlee poured much of his ill-gotten gains back into the black community. Greenlee created perhaps the best team—white or black—of all time: the Pittsburgh Crawfords. He spent lavishly on the team and, in 1932, constructed Greenlee Field, the first black-owned and -built ballpark in the nation. Then he signed Leroy "Satchel" Paige, the first Negro League player inducted into the Baseball Hall of Fame (whom many believe to be the greatest pitcher ever), and slugger Josh Gibson, one of baseball's best hitters and catchers. The 1936 version of the Crawfords included James "Cool Papa" Bell, Oscar Charleston, and William Julius (Judy) Johnson, all future Hall of Famers.[9] A reconstituted version of the Negro National League held its first All-Star Game in 1933, the same year the white major leagues began their own contest, and the black game routinely drew more fans.[10]

Regardless of their successes, the Negro Leagues labored under a cloud of impending doom. They were a source of pride, money, culture, and great play, but they also sowed the seeds of their own destruction by preparing black players for integration. For most blacks, the demise of segregated baseball was the ultimate goal. Jim Crow forced Negro Leaguers to accept inferior facilities; sometimes players had to dress elsewhere before playing in a white stadium. Salaries, even for the stars, were but a fraction of those earned by the average player in organized baseball. Discomfort accompanied the camaraderie, and discrimination

Figure 1. *The Negro League Era*

The great pitcher Satchel Paige (left) chats with teammate Jackie Robinson in 1945. Both men played for the Kansas City Monarchs of the Negro American League before Robinson was signed to a contract with the Montreal Royals in 1945. Paige debuted in the majors with the Cleveland Indians in 1948. In the inset, newly commissioned second lieutenant Jackie Robinson (right) stands with a fellow officer at Fort Riley, Kansas, in 1943. Robinson was reassigned to Fort Hood, Texas, shortly thereafter.

National Baseball Hall of Fame Library, Cooperstown, N.Y.

existed alongside the opportunity to play ball. Black ballplayers were practically invisible, forced into segregation and, for most, lost to history. While some seventy-two Negro Leaguers eventually made it to the major leagues, many more missed their chance.[11]

For those who qualified, integration would be a slow, fitful process. In 1933, an informal vote taken at the annual Baseball Writers' Association of America dinner showed that all but one white manager favored signing black players. Two years later, the Washington Senators signed Bobby Estalella, who "passed" as a dark-skinned Cuban player. Over the next few years, sportswriters lobbied for Senators owner Clark Griffith to sign Negro Leaguers. He reportedly contacted Buck Leonard and Josh Gibson but decided against disrupting the status quo of whites-only ball.

Tradition, based on deep-seated racial views of African Americans as inferior in sports, indeed, in all aspects of life, turned out to be the biggest barrier to integration. Most whites hardly considered the issue of a black man in baseball; after all, African Americans had their own leagues. Yet ironically, most white northerners did not seem opposed to baseball desegregation. Whenever surveyed, northern whites shrugged at the notion of black players in the major leagues. One salesman from the Bronx observed, "Colored men can enter almost any other field. Why not baseball?"[12] But the color line was deeply entrenched in the North as well as the South, as discrimination in housing, health care, and employment attested. Whites might have warmed to the idea of black stars playing for their teams, but they did not want them in their neighborhoods.

Baseball was pickled in traditional racism. Blacks and whites could not mix because that was the way things had always been. The ingrained racism of owners and executives intensified that attitude. To be sure, money could be made by tapping black communities that had grown as a result of the Great Migration, but a tradition of fear toward African Americans—coupled with white owners' fears that they would lose gate receipts if white spectators stayed away from games due to the presence of blacks—stalled progress toward integration.

Traditional racism, however, faced pressure from the press and civil rights activists. In 1931, the popular white columnist Westbrook Pegler opened an attack on the color line by ridiculing owners for their quiet gentleman's agreement to exclude blacks. In the early 1930s, black sportswriters formed a newspaper association to extol the great play of the Negro Leagues and promote integration. They had increasing leverage to do so because the black press had established itself as a mass forum for the African American community to express its views on civil rights. Despite the Depression, some 150 African American newspapers, with an average weekly circulation of 600,000, were in existence, and the number doubled by the eve of World War II.[13] Sam Lacy at the *Chicago Defender*, the *Pittsburgh Courier*'s Wendell Smith, Joe Bostic at the *New York Age* in Harlem, and "Doc" Kountze at the *Boston Chronicle* led the charge, themselves victims of segregation as they were often barred from press boxes. Joined by the Communist press (Document 1) and white commentators such as the dissident Pegler (Document 2), they denounced baseball's color line through the 1930s. The importance of their efforts cannot be understated, especially because baseball at this time was truly the nation's pastime, and print journalism and radio covered the game extensively. As a strike against Jim Crow in general, they believed, a press campaign to integrate organized baseball might transform white attitudes from apathy to receptivity.

Polling by black journalists showed that white players, managers, and executives in baseball did not publicly oppose integration. The president of the National League announced in 1933 that, according to league policy, race had no bearing on whether a player joined the major leagues. It was up to the owners to decide. As mentioned previously, many owners worried that white fans might balk when faced with black players and that they would refuse to attend games altogether if seated next to black fans, who were at the time either consigned to segregated sections or barred from ballparks. Other white owners took a different stance. Some of them rented parks to black teams and earned large sums operating the concessions at these parks. Observing the rich vein of talent in the Negro Leagues, they licked their chops at the skyrocketing receipts from these operations and dreamed of black players who might make their own teams winners and, thus, big attractions at the gate.

Black journalists understood the bottom line. They thought that a well-planned campaign, sensitive to public opinion but still forward-looking, might identify a player who had not only baseball talent but also the ability to withstand abuse, the calm demeanor to turn the other cheek, and the fortitude to stay the course. By the early 1940s, they saw Jackie Robinson as an obvious option, and they brought him to the attention of African American readers long before white America knew his name. He was educated, fiercely proud, and a great athlete. His well-publicized athletic achievements in college had already boosted him to a level of acceptance in white America. As the black press hammered away at the issue, it got a major boost from the Second World War, which transformed America—and baseball as well.

DOUBLE V: VICTORY OVER RACISM ABROAD AND AT HOME

Racism greatly shaped the epic conflict of World War II. The Japanese subjugated people in Asia based on their hierarchical conceptions of inferiority and viewed Americans as decadent white Westerners. For their part, U.S. soldiers engaged Japanese armies on racial terms, mystified by the seemingly fanatical behavior of their enemy. At home, the U.S. government imprisoned more than 110,000 people of Japanese descent in internment camps, a flagrant violation of civil rights. The Holocaust was the most infamous race-based crime of the war, but other groups joined the Nazis in persecuting people based on race and ethnicity, such as Italian Fascists' campaigns against African nations.

Even some scientific thinking, developed to justify nineteenth-century imperialism, promoted notions that dark-skinned people were inferior. These ideas carried into the American military, and the very armed forces that fought racism abroad discriminated against blacks among its own ranks. The U.S. Army and Navy, bolstered by an ingrained view of blacks as intellectually inferior, afraid of danger, and unable to take the initiative in combat, segregated blacks and whites. This segregation reflected the prejudice blacks faced in American society at large.

Nonetheless, the imperative of defeating racism abroad presented the hope that it could be defeated at home as well. With three-quarters of the nation's twelve million African Americans living in the Jim Crow South, blacks on the home front sought racial justice as payment for their support of the war as laborers in wartime factories. Returning black veterans took up that cause, too. As their race consciousness increased based on their experience of fighting Nazism and Japanese racism, they committed themselves to fighting white supremacy in America as well. Veterans and workers alike, joined by civil rights activists and social justice advocates, promoted the "Double V" campaign—victory over racism both overseas and at home. The effort hinged on presidential directives (in the absence of legislation) outlawing discrimination in the defense industry, the military, housing, the electoral process, and public places. As membership in the venerable NAACP skyrocketed and younger African Americans joined the Congress of Racial Equality (CORE), founded in 1942, civil rights activists turned to President Roosevelt for support.

To pressure the president the year before, labor union leader A. Philip Randolph and other activists threatened to organize a march on Washington, D.C., to protest discrimination. Roosevelt headed off the embarrassing march by issuing the first presidential order since Reconstruction to prohibit discrimination in employment practices by federal agencies, companies, and labor unions engaged in defense industries. Though a small step toward true racial justice—to the disappointment of civil rights leaders, the executive order did not ban segregation in the armed forces—it nonetheless opened up jobs to more than two million black workers in industry and government. African American membership in unions shot up during the war, from 200,000 to 1.25 million. By 1944, blacks accounted for 10 percent of the workforce, just slightly over their representation in the population as a whole at the time. Like Jackie Robinson after the war, black activists during it reflected the collective defiance of Americans who demanded civil rights for all.

Though not completely successful, the Double V campaign awakened America to the possibilities of transformation in race relations. Because of the dire need for manpower, the Army and Navy incrementally integrated selected facilities and units. In addition, nearly three-quarters of a million blacks migrated out of the South during the war, and 1.4 million left the South during the decade of the 1940s, bringing their campaign for integration into the more receptive North. Perhaps most crucial, the idea of creating a society truly based on pluralism, diversity, equality, and justice began to permeate the national dialogue. As a propaganda tool against Nazism—and, soon, Soviet tyranny—and as a way of questioning European imperialism in Africa and Asia, the American civil rights movement took on global significance. Gunnar Myrdal's seminal study, *An American Dilemma: The Negro Problem and Modern Democracy*, appeared in 1944 just as the United States stood poised for world leadership and as black veterans returned from the war with expectations of equal rights.

Myrdal, a Swedish economist and sociologist, concluded that racism afflicted the nation to its very core. White America's oppression of blacks led to their poor performance in society and thus confirmed whites' preconceived notion of African Americans as inferior. That vicious cycle was the American dilemma: White discrimination kept blacks in substandard conditions, thereby verifying white views that blacks had mediocre intelligence, questionable work habits, and low morals. Myrdal advocated a "creed" of fairness and equal rights to break the cycle. To be sure, conditions generally improved for blacks during the war, and ideas about an American creed of equality and democracy grew more prominent in reaction to the vicious race war. The need for black workers, alongside the moral thrust of the equal rights campaign, enhanced the push for better treatment. This was the context of Jackie Robinson's moment—a time ripe for baseball to seek a solution to the American dilemma of racism toward blacks.[14]

ROBINSON AT WAR

Jackie Robinson entered the U.S. Army in early April 1942. Sent to Fort Riley, Kansas, for basic training, he encountered Jim Crow firsthand. In his segregated cavalry unit, he was assigned to care for the horses, including mucking the stalls. Seeking better work, he was turned down for the base's Officer Candidate School—a supposedly race-neutral institution—until the famed heavyweight boxer Joe Louis interceded on his behalf. Robinson completed training at the school in January 1943 and was commissioned as a second lieutenant, but the several months' delay due to the machinations of racist policies raised his ire. He then tried to join the Fort Riley baseball squad, to play alongside future Dodgers teammates Pete Reiser and Dixie Walker, only to learn that the team was for whites only. There was no team for blacks. Gallingly, the base recruited Robinson for its football team, but he rejected the offer when told he could not play against teams from the South. Robinson developed a reputation as a hothead willing to stand up to Jim Crow. Joe Louis confirmed that Robinson "wouldn't take shit from anyone."[15] Irritated by Robinson's attitude, his white commanding officers sent him to Fort Hood, Texas, as a platoon leader in the segregated 761st Tank Battalion, known as the Black Panthers. The move boosted his baseball career because it prompted him to start playing again. It was not so good for his reputation, however.

On the evening of July 6, 1944, Robinson boarded a base bus and took a middle seat next to a fellow officer's wife, whom the driver mistook for a white woman. As throughout the South, buses were segregated at Fort Hood, with blacks expected to sit in the back. When Robinson refused to move, the driver shouted racial epithets. At the end of the line, after Robinson also confronted the investigating duty officer, military police took him into custody to face three counts of insubordination. Lobbied by the black press, Commander Paul Bates blocked Robinson's court-martial. Instead, Robinson was transferred to another battalion, whose top officer charged Robinson with additional offenses, including drunkenness (though he did not consume alcohol). Before his trial, Robinson defended himself in a letter to Assistant Secretary of War Truman K. Gibson (Document 3). He stood his ground on the witness stand, explaining his visceral response to the word *nigger* and invoking the memory of his grandmother, a slave, who "said the definition of the word was a low, uncouth person, and pertains to no one in particular; but I don't consider that I am low and uncouth."[16] An all-white panel of officers acquitted Robinson, who was eventually mustered out of the military with an honorable discharge in November 1944 due to a physical disability (a bad ankle), which conveniently allowed the Army to sidestep the racism issue. Although he did exit as an officer, the military was no road to racial equality for Jackie Robinson.

Just before his discharge, Robinson wrote to the Kansas City Monarchs baseball club to ask for a tryout. The Monarchs, one of the elite Negro League squads, had lost much of their talent to the war. A nationally known athlete, Robinson could fill an important gap for the struggling team. Agreeing to a $400 per month contract (a good sum that reflected his fan appeal), Robinson played shortstop for the Monarchs in forty-seven games in 1945. To the satisfaction of the black press, he hit .387 and had 5 home runs and 13 stolen bases. Robinson was less than thrilled, however, by the league's disorganization and hectic travel schedule, which kept him apart from his fiancée, Rachel Isum, whom he had met while both were students at UCLA. But just as the war provided an opportunity for African Americans to launch the Double V campaign, Robinson's performance with the Monarchs boosted their drive to break the color barrier in organized baseball.

BASEBALL AND WORLD WAR II

When asked about the possibility of blacks joining the major leagues in 1944, Commissioner Kenesaw Mountain Landis refused to act, announcing that the matter was closed. Nonetheless, the tide was running against those still mired in Jim Crow practices. Rising support for the integration of baseball emerged from a general unease with segregation, in part fueled by the Double V campaign, and from the desire to field the best teams possible. Chicago Cubs owner William Wrigley Jr. predicted that integration was imminent, but other executives would not budge. (Wrigley was often ahead of the curve. To stem the loss of players due to the wartime draft, he organized the All-American Girls Professional Baseball League in 1943, which drew fans in midwestern cities.) In the spring of 1943, the Los Angeles and Oakland clubs in the Pacific Coast League announced their intention to try out a few black players, but both teams reneged. In response, unions opposed to discrimination picketed the Los Angeles Angels' opening day game.

By 1944, politicians also took note. When Landis died that year, the new commissioner, a former U.S. senator from Kentucky named Albert Benjamin "Happy" Chandler, hinted that it was time to overcome the color barrier. Some owners agreed but only intimated their leanings. The New York State legislature passed a law prohibiting discrimination in employment on the basis of color. The owners got the message: Without action of their own, the legislature would make doing business a burden for the Brooklyn Dodgers, and New York Giants and Yankees. In August 1944, New York City mayor Fiorello La Guardia, an energetic, progressive champion of immigrants and ethnic minorities, appointed the Mayor's Committee on Baseball to investigate racial segregation in baseball. In August 1945, the committee issued its report, which recommended that the major leagues integrate as quickly as possible but left the process of doing so to each club (Document 4). The tradition of prejudice was again holding up the integration of baseball.

In early 1945, a Jewish city councilman in Boston, Isadore Muchnick, threatened to revoke the license that permitted the hometown Braves and Red Sox to play on Sunday unless they allowed blacks to play. "I cannot understand how baseball," he wrote both teams' owners, "which claims to be the national sport and which in my opinion receives special favors and dispensations from the Federal Government because of alleged morale value, can continue a pre–Civil War attitude toward American citizens because of the color of their skin."[17] The "special favors" to which Muchnick referred included a "green light" message in 1942 from President Roosevelt to Commissioner Landis to play ball rather than shut down the leagues, despite the war emergency, because the sport boosted workers' morale and symbolized American stability in an uncertain world. That sentiment, driven home by the Double V campaign, brought baseball in line with the fight against racism abroad.

As Muchnick continued to press, black journalists did, too. In April 1945, as Robinson debuted with the Monarchs, journalist Joe Bostic in New York encountered the key white figure in the campaign for integration: Branch Rickey, president and general manager of the Brooklyn Dodgers. Bostic visited the Dodgers' training camp with two aging Negro Leaguers. Rickey, who among major league baseball executives was the one who most leaned toward integrating African Americans into the sport (and was familiar with Myrdal's *An American Dilemma*), dismissed them and lashed out privately at Bostic for putting him on the spot. Meanwhile, Wendell Smith of the nation's most prestigious African American newspaper, the *Pittsburgh Courier*, began reporting on Robinson's baseball exploits in Kansas City, apparently to encourage another tryout by a Negro League player. Smith emerged as a vigorous advocate for baseball integration among the black press; this former athlete claimed to have entered journalism to fight Jim Crow in baseball.[18]

Smith and Councilman Muchnick arrived in Boston with Robinson and two other Negro League stars, Sam Jethroe and Marvin Williams, to meet with the Red Sox front office. Robinson was decidedly the inferior player of the three, but he was also a veteran, a college man, the oldest (at twenty-six), and the most articulate. Thus Smith sought to elevate his profile. The Red Sox balked, waiting four days before letting the three on the field on April 16. They impressed the coaches, but the few onlookers, comprised mostly of management, shouted curses from the stands. After filling out applications for employment, the three never heard from Boston again. Furious, the black press protested that the episode had humiliated the African American race. Robinson also expressed his disdain.

Despite the setback, Wendell Smith met with Branch Rickey, who indicated that he sought the appropriate black player to test the waters of integration. Although not the determining factor in Rickey's calculations, the black press remained pivotal in the integration of organized baseball because Rickey often leaked information to key black sportswriters before going public in the mainstream white newspapers. Rickey met Robinson for the first time in June 1945, when the Monarchs played in Newark, New Jersey, and the Dodgers executive was impressed by Robinson's clean lifestyle and desire to avoid his carousing teammates. And Robinson could play, though by no means was he the best in the Negro Leagues. He was erratic in the field, but he could hit on occasion, and he certainly had speed on the bases, which excited the crowds. During an August 1945 exhibition game against the Navy All-Stars in Boston, Robinson stole home, a move that became his trademark. Two weeks after the Japanese surrender, on August 14, 1945, finally ended the Second World War, Branch Rickey invited Robinson to meet with him, in effect merging the Double V campaign with organized baseball.

BRANCH RICKEY'S STEPS TO INTEGRATION

When the paunchy, flamboyant sixty-three-year old Rickey called in Robinson for an interview, the process of erasing the color line became a determined effort. Rickey had served for three decades in the front offices of the St. Louis Browns and Cardinals. After making his mark by developing an early form of the "farm system," which used the minor leagues to train and season future major leaguers, he became general manager, president, and one-third owner of the Brooklyn Dodgers in 1942. Rickey's ambition and shrewdness led him to Jackie Robinson.

A showman who spouted biblical passages, Rickey disguised his penurious ways and desire for profit with reverential expressions of morality.[19] He had made a fortune for the Cardinals as well as himself, and black talent could augment his bottom line by transforming his struggling Dodgers into a powerhouse. Revenue and profits would pour in, as fans in greater numbers than ever before would pay to see Brooklyn win. Rickey would be the king of the baseball world, and his Dodgers would supplant the Cardinals as the chief contender for the National League pennant. His drive for fortune aside, Rickey was a religious man, a Methodist who believed that morality went hand in hand with making money. At a time when Americans seemed ready to embrace desegregation, he sent scouts to observe the Negro Leagues and identify a black player to be the test case for his move to integrate baseball.

Rickey sought someone who was a star on the field and a mature, tough man off it, someone who could endure racial slights. But if his self-proclaimed, multiyear effort to find the right man was accurate, why take an aging former football player who had a suspect throwing arm and bat as well as a record of confronting racism rather than backing away? The answer: The black press had already identified Robinson as one of the best candidates to change baseball and boost Rickey's profit margin.

Rickey masterfully laid the groundwork before he invited Robinson to chat. He disguised his scouting trips to avoid scaring off other owners and the commissioner by claiming that he was recruiting players for his Brooklyn Brown Dodgers, a team in the new United States Baseball League, which Rickey had established as a means to try out black players in front of white audiences. In tandem with Wendell Smith, Rickey scripted the sports story of the century, which Smith would break to the public on a carefully calculated date after Rickey met with Robinson.

At the historic interview of August 28, 1945, Robinson expected to be signed to a Brown Dodgers contract, but Rickey soon showed his cards. He wanted Robinson to sign with the white Dodgers and become the man who would erase the national pastime's color line (Document 5). Shouting insults that Robinson would face, the theatrical Rickey role-played taunting fans, insensitive managers, and racist, spike-sliding players. "Mr. Rickey," asked Robinson, "do you want a ballplayer who's not afraid to fight back?" No, replied the Dodgers president, "I want a

Figure 2. *The Signing*

In 1950, Jackie Robinson and Branch Rickey reenact the contract signing of April 10, 1947 (at which the Dodgers manager, Burt Shotton, was also present), which allowed the first African American to play in the major leagues since the 1880s.

National Baseball Hall of Fame Library, Cooperstown, N.Y.

ballplayer with guts enough *not* to fight back."[20] Rickey would not blame Robinson if he responded by "coming up swinging," but, he warned, "that would set the cause back twenty years."[21]

To drive home the point about nonresistance as a means of change, the Methodist Rickey gave the deeply religious Robinson a copy of a current bestseller, *Life of Christ*, by Giovanni Papini, and instructed him to read the passages on avoiding confrontations.[22] A few years before, the ballplayer had learned from his girlfriend, Rachel, to temper some of his rage through prayer. But he also believed that being Christian did not mean he had to be submissive on the issue of racism. Handing Robinson the book by Papini, Rickey reminded him of Jesus's words: "Resist not evil: but whosoever shall smite thee on thy right cheek, turn to him the other also."[23]

Robinson signed a contract for $600 a month, plus a decent $3,500 bonus, to play for Brooklyn's top minor league club, the Montreal Royals, in 1946. The contract was signed in private, as Rickey wanted to prevent outside pressure—whether from angry whites or black militants—from undermining his orchestrated effort at integration. He also wanted to give Robinson at least a year in Montreal to prepare for the ordeal of integration.

But word got out, and the signing, repeated publicly on October 23, created shock waves in the baseball world and made headlines throughout the country. Coverage in the mainstream media was largely calm and restrained (Documents 6 and 7), but the black press exultantly treated the news as a blow to Jim Crow (Document 8). Polls showed that most major leaguers, even from the South, were willing to give Robinson a chance—as long as he did not join their clubs. By the end of 1945, organized baseball was largely resigned to the inevitable. There was no logic in keeping blacks out of the major leagues, especially after they had served bravely in World War II. In early 1946, moreover, the National Football League ended its ban on black players. The national pastime was expected to follow suit.

A BLACK MAN IN BASEBALL

Robinson married Rachel Isum in February 1946, and two weeks later the newlyweds headed for the Royals' spring training camp in Daytona Beach, Florida. The trip south was humiliating, however, as the Robinsons were bumped from several airline flights because they were black.

In the meantime, Rickey signed another African American player named Johnny Wright to keep Robinson company.

As camp began, in Sanford, Florida, the police chief pledged to enforce a local law that prohibited integrated play by canceling games if Robinson appeared. He and Wright, a twenty-seven-year-old former Negro League pitcher, were removed from an early contest, against the protests of the national media, when the police chief made good on his word. Robinson then threatened to leave the team when he discovered that his accommodations in Sanford were also dictated by Jim Crow. That is, he could not get accommodations equal to those of his white teammates and had to stay in the black section of town—but Wendell Smith persuaded him to stay. After relenting, Robinson said that Sanford "wasn't a bad town at all" and that the people were simply curious over his appearance.[24] He turned the other cheek, as Rickey had demanded. Worried about Robinson, the Dodgers president also signed Roy Campanella, Don Newcombe, and Roy Partlow to contracts, hoping that at least one of the five black players would succeed.

Unlike their minor league affiliate, the Royals, the Dodgers did not have their own training facility in Daytona Beach, so the team relied on fields in the area that were subject to local race ordinances. While white civic leaders in the Daytona Beach area pledged to cooperate to mitigate racial tensions, cities such as Jacksonville (where the Dodgers had trained for years prior to 1946) prohibited African Americans from playing with whites. Under protest from the Dodgers and facing criticism in northern cities, Jacksonville officials simply canceled exhibition games rather than mix the races on the field (and, potentially, in the stands). In Deland, a game was called off ostensibly due to an electrical malfunction. The truth was that prejudice had prevailed (Document 9). Ultimately, even the Royals moved their camp to a black section of Daytona Beach. But Rickey warned all 150 players in Florida that he would not tolerate discrimination.

Staring down Jim Crow at Daytona Beach's City Island Ball Park on March 17, 1946, in an exhibition between the Royals and their big league affiliate, the Dodgers, Robinson became the first black player since Moses Fleetwood Walker in 1888 to take the field against a major league team. But he did not fare particularly well during the preseason, and some commentators questioned his credentials and accused him of receiving special treatment.

The Royals opened the regular season of the International League (a Triple-A division one step below the major leagues) on April 18 in Jersey City, New Jersey, marking Robinson's professional debut. Stepping up his game, he performed brilliantly, getting four hits in five plate appearances, including a home run. The black press was ecstatic (Document 10), and fans turned out in droves to watch him play. During the 1946 season, in which he won the International League's batting title and was voted Most Valuable Player, more than a million spectators paid to see Robinson. Rickey was content with his experiment, so far.

Despite the accolades, Robinson faced hostility everywhere he went. An exhibition tour through the South was canceled due to threats. A brawl erupted in Baltimore, where white spectators barricaded Robinson in the clubhouse until 1:00 a.m., screaming, "Come out here Robinson, you son of a bitch. We're gonna get you."[25] Such blatant displays of racism were not confined to the South. In Buffalo, New York, Bisons players spiked him as they slid into second base, knocking him out of the lineup for three weeks. Back in Montreal, to counter the tough treatment he received on the road, his supporters roared their approval, particularly when the team played the visiting Louisville Colonels, whose fans had so abused Robinson when the Royals played in the city. Rumors that he would quit and that Rickey was souring on him dogged Robinson. His pregnant wife felt his burden, but he remained stoic—and focused. Gratifyingly, he led Montreal to victory in the Little (or Junior) World Series, the minor league title, against the despised Louisville Colonels.

Inspired by Robinson, and continuing its decades-long crusade for racial justice, the NAACP continued to picket hotels that barred black players, protested in cities that upheld segregation in baseball, and urged baseball clubs to integrate (Document 11). Baseball owners themselves continued to deliberate over integration throughout 1946, ultimately concluding not to allow outsiders with political motives, who cared little about the sport, to pressure them into letting African Americans play in the major leagues (Document 12). With the topic of race prominent in the news, Robinson tried to keep a low profile. In the off-season, he played with the touring all-black Kansas City Monarchs, but he was unable to shake the open secret that he would be brought up to the major leagues.

The debate persisted over whether Negro Leaguers were good enough to play in the majors or whether they would simply be given a pass for ethical reasons. The so-called "bible of baseball," the *Sporting News*, remained antagonistic to integration. Cleveland Indians pitching ace Bob "Rapid Robert" Feller remarked that only Satchel Paige was qualified for the big leagues. Feller had qualms about Robinson, arguing that he was too muscle-bound from football to hit effectively. "If he were a white man," alleged the future Hall of Famer, "I doubt if they would consider him big league material."[26] Yet Feller, like most other players, believed the time for integration had come (Document 13).

Rickey persevered. In January 1947, the owners discreetly met to discuss the race question. Of the sixteen executives, all but Rickey (who represented the Dodgers) backed segregation, even though the ballot was secret. To bypass his fellow magnates, Rickey got Commissioner Chandler's assurance that the league would approve Robinson's contract. Rickey then approached black leaders in Brooklyn. He asked them to dissuade African American fans from strutting, parading, and holding "Jackie Robinson Days" or other distractions that might characterize baseball integration as a victory for blacks over whites. Always skeptical of white assurances regarding civil rights (Document 14), black leaders nonetheless agreed. They promised a campaign called "Don't Spoil Jackie's Chances" that would urge African Americans to cooperate and not provoke whites. Meanwhile, a still cautious Rickey prompted Robinson to withdraw from speaking engagements on behalf of the Detroit Committee to Fight Racial Injustice and Terrorism. To avoid a stir at the Dodgers' spring training camp in 1947 in Cuba (since they could not play in segregated Florida), Rickey moved Robinson, Partlow, Campanella, and Newcombe (Johnny Wright was no longer with the team) to a seedy hotel, while the white players resided at the lush Hotel Nacional. Even though the latter hotel was integrated, Rickey explained to an infuriated Robinson the need to circumvent a racial incident by separating black and white players off the field.

With Robinson set to play first base, Rickey's scheme then encountered its biggest challenge to date. As the team moved to Panama to play some exhibition games in March 1947, some of the southern players, led by the popular right fielder Dixie Walker, circulated a petition saying that they would not play with Robinson. Rickey immediately ordered the fiery Dodgers manager, Leo Durocher, to call a midnight team meeting. "Leo the Lip," as he was known, berated the white players. He told them that, as manager, only he decided who would play, that Robinson could make them all rich, and that he would trade any dissenters to another team. "I don't care if a guy is yellow or black, or if he has stripes like a fuckin' zebra," the bombastic Durocher declared.[27] So ended the mutiny—and indeed, by the close of the 1947 season, all six of the southern troublemakers were gone from the team.

But confusion set in during early April as the major league season neared. A sickly Robinson did not play well in Panama, and he was then sidelined after a collision on the base paths. Robinson remained determined to succeed, but he spoke out about his frustrations in the black press (Document 15). Durocher, meanwhile, received news of his suspension for the entire 1947 season due to squabbling with Yankees president Larry MacPhail, and scout Clyde Sukeforth temporarily took over the team. The press speculated on Robinson's fate: Would he be called up to the Dodgers or remain with the Royals? On April 10, Robinson returned to the dugout to learn that Rickey had released a statement to the press: "The Brooklyn Dodgers today purchased the contract of Jackie Roosevelt Robinson from the Montreal Royals. He will report immediately." Two days later, picking up his uniform with the number 42, Robinson reported to Ebbets Field as the first black man to sign a major league contract in the twentieth century (Documents 16 and 17).

Robinson's signing turned the national pastime into a social laboratory. On April 15, 1947, the first African American to play in an official major league baseball game took the field against the Boston Braves. Robinson went hitless that day in a 5–3 Dodgers hometown win; in fact, he did not record a hit in his first twenty times at bat over the next five games. His mediocre play was immaterial, however. By stepping onto Ebbets Field that day, he became a civil rights pioneer on America's long trek toward "a more perfect Union."

During the first season of integrated major league baseball, race and racism were always in the background (Documents 18–21). Famed broadcaster Red Barber later noted that 1947 was the year "when all hell broke loose" because of integration. While the season progressed without chaos, baseball showed America a glimpse of its desegregated future, and Jackie Robinson was the agent of change.[28]

The black press remained proud, and black and white fans alike cheered Robinson and his impact. In truth, though, while he affected attendance at home and away in 1947, the rise in spectators was also due to overall interest in the sport and America's growing postwar affluence. He never had the impact on ticket sales that had been Rickey's major impetus for benching Jim Crow in the first place.[29] The Dodgers' home attendance increased that season, but by a mere eleven thousand fans, and it actually declined as a percentage of total National League attendance. In the ensuing years, attendance overall actually dropped, even at Ebbets Field. Indeed, the Dodgers never climbed above their 1947 attendance totals until they left for Los Angeles eleven years later (Document 22). And ironically, black fans might have made up for a decline in the number of white fans because many whites were uncomfortable sitting with African Americans at games, and so stayed away.

But it was Robinson's transformation of the game itself that year — creating the opportunity for blacks to enter organized baseball — that mattered. In July, center fielder Larry Doby of the Cleveland Indians became the first black player in the American League. The next year, catcher Roy Campanella joined the Dodgers, and then more Negro Leaguers (such as Satchel Paige) joined the major league ranks. Baseball integration made teams more competitive. Winners—such as the New York teams of the National League in the 1940s and 1950s, with their black players—hoped to attract more and more fans by desegregation, though this was not necessarily the case.

Robinson was the first African American player, however, and he endured a baptism of racist fire in 1947. The St. Louis Cardinals, for instance, planned to strike instead of playing against Robinson. National League president Ford Frick nipped that rebellion in the bud by threatening to suspend any player who refused to take the field. "This is the United States of America," declared Frick, "and one citizen has as much right to play as another. The National League will go down the line with Robinson no matter what the consequences."[30] The Cardinals were rough with him on the field, though, as he became once more the target of spiked slides (one of which opened a seven-inch-long cut in his leg) after he shifted to playing second base, his permanent position. In Cincinnati, the FBI was so worried about death threats that they checked the neighborhood surrounding the ballpark for snipers (Document 23). Threats against Robinson, his wife, and his infant son, Jackie Jr., persisted. As Rachel listened to the verbal abuse from the stands, she determined to "sit up very straight, as if my back could absorb the nefarious outbursts and prevent them from reaching him."[31]

Her efforts failed. In Philadelphia, manager Ben Chapman, a Tennessee native, mercilessly catcalled from the bench, and Phillies players followed his lead: "Hey, nigger, why don't you go back to the cotton field where you belong?" and "Snowflake, which one of those white boys' wives are you dating tonight?"[32] Chapman claimed that he always heckled rookies; "bench jockeys" were an accepted part of the game. That was true, but Chapman's abuse was extreme. Even Alabama native Dixie Walker, who had led the aborted Dodgers rebellion, criticized the manager. Under pressure from the press, Frick ordered Chapman to cease the verbal harangues. Robinson, having pledged to Rickey to turn the other cheek, even agreed to pose for a photograph with Chapman (Document 24). In retirement, however, he confessed that he had come very close to smashing in the teeth of his tormentor.

For his part, Robinson was a sensation on the field. The Dodgers won the National League pennant, and Robinson was named Major League

Figure 3. *The Robinson Trademark*
Robinson is tagged out at home plate by catcher Clyde McCullough of the
Chicago Cubs on May 2, 1951, at Ebbets Field. Robinson terrified pitchers
with his quickness on the base paths. He became famous for his ability to
steal home—a feat that requires daring and aggressiveness, because the pitch
arrives before the runner—which he did nineteen times in his career (tied for
ninth all-time).
National Baseball Hall of Fame Library, Cooperstown, N.Y.

Rookie of the Year, an award that at the time was given to the best first-
year player in both leagues. Unfortunately for the millions who sought
a Hollywood ending to the year's biggest sports story, the Yankees prevailed over the Dodgers in a thrilling seven-game World Series.

Over the next two years, as baseball slowly integrated, the pressure on Robinson eased a bit. His teammates, other players, and the
public rallied around the second baseman when they heard the taunts.
The popular shortstop Pee Wee Reese, who had grown up in racially

segregated Louisville, Kentucky, but had refused to sign Walker's petition, in particular befriended Robinson. In 1948, Reese responded to racial slurs from a Cincinnati crowd with an intentionally public display of chatting with Robinson.

Beyond his teammates, minority groups rallied to Robinson's cause, including the Jewish community. Although on occasion antagonistic toward each other, blacks and Jews had a mutual interest in integration, and Jewish journalists and leaders were important to the Jackie Robinson story.[33] The popularity of baseball in this demographic was so substantial that in the first half of the twentieth century, owners and managers in cities where Jews were concentrated, such as New York, searched for talented Jewish ballplayers. In 1941, the Giants had four Jewish players on the team.

Baseball is a game of numbers, and great statistics are immune to biased interpretation. In the 1930s and 1940s, the performance of Detroit Tigers slugger and first baseman Hank Greenberg revolutionized mainstream thinking about Jews in baseball. Nonetheless, Greenberg, the first Jewish superstar ballplayer (and later the first Jew elected to the Hall of Fame), encountered anti-Semitism on the field. There were rumors that his attempt to surpass Babe Ruth's single-season home run record of 60 fell short (Greenberg ended up with 58) because organized baseball could not tolerate having a Jew break the revered Ruth's record. During Robinson's rookie season, Greenberg, at the tail end of his career, befriended Robinson. For instance, in May 1947, after the two collided during a game, the next time Robinson reached first base, Greenberg asked him if he was hurt. Thereafter, Robinson had a deep respect for Greenberg. Like Greenberg, many Jews, as fellow victims of discrimination, felt a kinship with Robinson (Document 25).

Indeed, spectators from around the country issued expressions of support, sympathy, and even love for Robinson (Document 26). A white man from Richmond, Virginia, wanted him "to know that not all of us southerners are SOBs."[34] A "White Boy" from Portland, Oregon, addressed him as "Black Boy" and told him, "You are a credit to your race—the human race, son. Very glad to see you in the Majors."[35] A beauty contest winner asked for a date. Over the next nine seasons, although the flow of hate mail continued, so did the support and acclaim. The Rickey-Robinson experiment was a victory for civil rights, African Americans, and the United States as a whole (Document 27).

Yet even as other professional and collegiate athletic organizations began to integrate, though slowly, some still resisted (Documents 28

Figure 4. *A Great Experiment*
Breaking the color barrier in the national pastime had symbolic importance
well beyond the baseball field. Robinson's achievement inspired hope for racial
integration in all areas of American life.
National Baseball Hall of Fame Library, Cooperstown, N.Y.

and 29). Before the 1949 season, Rickey canceled the requirement for
Robinson to remain passive in the face of abuse. Robinson responded
with the brashness of his college days. While playing brilliantly, he now
pledged to give as good as he got when it came to rough play, and he
did so by standing up to umpires and opposing players. The pride he
instilled in the black community was immense. Robinson garnered
accolades from such famous figures as musician Count Basie, who later
performed a version of a song about the player (Document 30), and in a
national poll in 1947, Robinson was named the most popular American

figure behind Bing Crosby. As the most visible African American in the United States, he also became a spokesman for civil rights.

FIGHTING FOR CIVIL RIGHTS IN A COLD WAR WORLD

Robinson's stature guaranteed his prominence in the campaign for civil rights, a movement that, in 1948, got a big boost from the president of the United States. Harry Truman, a Missourian who entered the civil rights battleground in reaction to the rising conflict, was disgusted by the violence blacks faced throughout the South. Lynching epitomized this murderous oppression, spurred by white supremacist reactions to returning black soldiers who campaigned for the Double V campaign and boosted voter rolls. Upon hearing details of these outrages, the appalled but politically pragmatic Truman—who sought the black vote for his reelection in 1948 while fearing the power of southern segregationists—in December 1946 created the President's Committee on Civil Rights to investigate the criminal behavior and issue recommendations.

The committee's 178-page report, released in October 1947 and titled *To Secure These Rights*, called for sweeping federal authority to desegregate the armed forces, interstate transportation, and government employment and to combat racial inequality through economic aid and protection against lynching and voting discrimination. The document recommended a special division in the Justice Department to prosecute civil rights violations and a permanent Commission on Civil Rights to continue to examine problems. In a special message to Congress on Civil Rights in February 1948, Truman announced his intention to back up *To Secure These Rights* with actions (Document 31). Truman survived a challenge from racist southern Democrats (Dixiecrats) to win a stunning victory in the 1948 election, thanks in part to the black vote. Surely, Robinson, who was undergoing a trial on the baseball field, appreciated the president's efforts on behalf of civil rights off the field.

In a way, Robinson reciprocated by standing up to communism—another Truman crusade—at the height of the cold war. In July 1949, the House Un-American Activities Committee (HUAC) called on him to testify regarding recent pro-Soviet remarks made by the black singer, actor, and human rights activist Paul Robeson. In 1943, Robeson had addressed Commissioner Landis and the owners on segregation in baseball; this appeal had followed on the heels of writer Lester Rodney's repeated denunciations of Jim Crow in the sport in the U.S. Communist party newspaper, the *Daily Worker*. Although Robeson never identified himself as a Communist, his unrestrained statements in praise of the Soviet Union, criticism of American racial policies, and belief that pressure from abroad would help end Jim Crow at home merged in a speech, remarkable for its strident tone and the publicity it earned, in April 1949 before two thousand delegates to the Congress of World Partisans of Peace in Paris.[36] Robeson's embrace of Moscow converted this famous entertainer into a prime suspect of the Communist-hunting HUAC.

Black opinion toward Robeson and the left was complicated. African Americans welcomed efforts by the U.S. Communist party on behalf of civil rights and economic aid, but they also embraced the American ideals of democracy and freedom, and by no means were they necessarily opposed to capitalism. By the time of Robinson's appearance before HUAC, the cold war had so magnified the threat of communism that blacks, like other citizens, felt compelled to take sides in the ideological struggle. Anti-Communist "Red Scare" hysteria had not only terrified labor unions, as the government hunted for supposed subversives, but also had led opponents of civil rights to paint supporters as deviants who threatened the American way of life. Ultimately, the cold war undercut the more radical crusade for economic and social justice, and the august NAACP banned Communists from its ranks.[37]

Still, the discrimination African Americans experienced was partly responsible for galvanizing Truman to protect the rights of minorities as part of a greater goal of upholding democratic values. Although his efforts to push through civil rights legislation in 1949 were stymied, again, by southern obstructionists in Congress, Truman earned the appreciation of African Americans for the effort. To be sure, he prioritized the cold war over civil rights. Because he needed southern votes to endorse national security measures, such as the Marshall Plan of aid to postwar Europe and the NATO military pact, America remained vulnerable to Soviet charges that, considering the widespread exclusion of blacks from the voting process, the United States did not practice the democracy and freedom it preached.

Thus, before the House Un-American Activities Committee on July 18, 1949, Robinson criticized the notion, as expressed by Robeson, that blacks embraced the Soviet Union, while he identified racial discrimination as un-American a practice as communism (Document 32). HUAC and the NAACP both applauded Robinson for his remarks. Yet many African Americans were uncomfortable with the idea that HUAC had pitted two black leaders against each other.

Irony abounded in Robinson's HUAC appearance. Although he had been called to testify in favor of American values, he was forced to leave the nation's capital immediately after his testimony because Jim Crow laws prohibited him from staying in Washington, D.C.'s white hotels. And while HUAC energetically investigated communism, the committee, unsurprisingly, never scrutinized homegrown fascists or the Ku Klux Klan.

Robeson, for his part, praised Robinson for his appearance, acknowledging the pressure on the ballplayer to testify and encouraging him to speak out for civil rights. This was the cold war, however, and while Robinson was identified with capitalism and democracy, Robeson was linked to Communist evil. African Americans were, therefore, forced to choose one or the other. Most in the mainstream black community sided with Robinson, although they were disappointed that he had conflated Communist ideology with militant black protest (even though that was not his intention).

Robinson later regretted the remarks that placed him in conflict with another black man and rendered him a representative of the cold war establishment. In his autobiography, *I Never Had It Made*, published in 1973, the year after his death, he admitted that he had much less faith in white justice later in life than he had in 1949 (Document 40). In fact, following his HUAC testimony, the FBI—which had earlier tried to protect him from death threats—opened a file on him to keep abreast of his affiliations with civil rights groups. This surveillance persisted until his death.[38]

RETIREMENT, RACE, AND SPORTS AT MID-CENTURY

Jackie Robinson's fortunes in baseball continued to soar into the 1950s. It was not until 1955 that he had a truly down year. By then, Robinson was thirty-six years old and in obvious decline. Because of his diminishing abilities, the team tried him at third base and in the outfield, and he was even benched for the deciding seventh game of the World Series, which the Dodgers won for the first time in their history that year. Traded to the New York Giants after the 1956 season, Robinson retired from baseball before the contract went into effect.

In 1962, his first year of eligibility, he was elected to the Baseball Hall of Fame, becoming the first African American inducted. Although his pathbreaking achievement in erasing the color line was the main reason he was so honored, Robinson also had amassed an impressive résumé as a ballplayer that merited his election. In his ten seasons in the majors, the Dodgers had gone to the World Series six times. He was an

All-Star in six of those years as well. His career batting average of .311, combined with high slugging and on-base percentages and a total of 197 stolen bases (including 19 steals of home), placed him in an elite group of players.

By the mid-1950s, though, the impact of his achievement on the baseball world was ambiguous. More than 150 blacks were playing in organized baseball (major and minor leagues), yet no teams or executives from the Negro Leagues had entered the majors. Even a request by the Negro Leagues to be considered as an elite minor league was rejected. At best, black teams were struggling, and even the most profitable among them, the Kansas City Monarchs, Robinson's former team, were in trouble financially. By this point, with the civil rights movement generating momentum, there was no interest in watching, much less remembering, Jim Crow–era baseball. That the Negro Leagues had been one of the biggest, most significant black-owned and -operated African American enterprises in the United States was forgotten. Democracy, ironically, had killed black baseball: An African American, wrote Wendell Smith, had walked in the door of the big leagues, and black baseball had walked out.[39]

The passing of the Negro Leagues did not deter Robinson in his business and civil rights ambitions. He was named the first black vice president of a major corporation, the Chock full o'Nuts coffee company, in 1957, and he served in that position and as director of personnel until 1964. He also joined the board of directors of the NAACP, heading the organization's Freedom Fund Drive. He promoted black-owned businesses and banks, and in 1970 he established the Jackie Robinson Construction Company to build low-income housing. Along the way, he also dabbled as a baseball announcer, becoming in 1965 the first African American to work as a television analyst for a major sportscast, ABC's *Major League Baseball Game of the Week.*

In the sports world, the barriers against minority athletes continued to fall—but slowly, and in fits and starts. By 1955, only the Washington Redskins held out against hiring black players in the National Football League.[40] The National Basketball Association finally admitted black players—Chuck Cooper, Nat Clifton, and Earl Lloyd—in 1950–1951. Just after the war, collegiate football witnessed enrollments of African American players as well, although they were prohibited from taking the field throughout the South. Three universities in the Southwest Conference remained segregated until 1970.[41] Even professional tennis and golf, with their white country-club roots, saw the color barrier fall in the two decades after the war.

Robinson had instigated a seismic shift in sports, but the legal system caused an even bigger earthquake in American society at large. In 1954, in the ruling *Brown v. Board of Education*, the U.S. Supreme Court struck down the "separate but equal" doctrine enshrined in *Plessy v. Ferguson* to declare segregation in public schools unconstitutional. Throughout the South, officials refused to integrate, dragging their heels in a show of massive resistance to the Court. In early September 1957, Congress passed the first civil rights act since Reconstruction, but implementation focused mainly on voter registration (and meagerly at that). Later that month, President Dwight Eisenhower ordered federal troops to Little Rock, Arkansas, to escort nine black students into Central High School after the NAACP had filed for a court decree to desegregate the schools. Faced with a recalcitrant governor, who mustered the National Guard against the students, and raging mobs of angry whites, the students turned to Eisenhower for help. Although the president responded, he counseled patience on the part of civil rights proponents. The following spring, Jackie Robinson sent a letter to Eisenhower urging more aggressive action, and immediately so (Document 33).

Two years later, when civil rights leader Martin Luther King Jr. was jailed in Albany, Georgia, Robinson called Republican presidential candidate Richard Nixon to ask for federal intervention or Nixon's personal attention, but he was rebuffed. Nonetheless, Robinson supported Nixon for the presidency in 1960, as he thought John F. Kennedy, the eventual winner in the election, too timid on civil rights. To show support for King, Robinson marched with him in Birmingham, Alabama, in 1962, a protest that shocked the nation when police attacked demonstrators with clubs, fire hoses, and dogs. When Mississippi NAACP leader Medgar Evers, a target of white supremacists, was gunned down in June 1963, Robinson telegrammed the White House to urge Kennedy — who had finally announced his support for civil rights legislation on television just hours before the killing — to act decisively to end Jim Crow (Document 34).

Not all activists lent blanket support to Robinson and his approach to securing civil rights. The black radical Malcolm X called Robinson an appeaser of his oppressors, especially in light of his testimony against Paul Robeson before HUAC years before. The militant Black Power leader accused Robinson of being a "house slave" who sold out the civil rights movement at the bidding of his "White Bosses" by helping to destroy Robeson and by endorsing Republican politicians.[42] For his part, Robinson accused Malcolm X of being destructive, sensationalist, and anti-Semitic, and of playing into the hands of white racists who would use Malcolm's words to scare white moderates (Document 35).

Rather than being a separatist, Robinson was an integrationist. He believed that blacks could assimilate into white culture if only America permitted them to do so. He was a uniter and a moderate on race relations (Document 36), but he had no patience with racism. Robinson, therefore, encouraged young black militant leaders to assail the bastions of racial prejudice. The FBI kept tabs on his support of the Black Panther Party for Self-Defense, a militant group that practiced what Malcolm X preached by showing a willingness to confront the white establishment through violent means if necessary. In July 1968, the Bureau added to its file on Robinson his statement to the press that the Black Panthers actually sought peace. Robinson was referring to a specific incident at the Brooklyn Criminal Courts Building the previous September, when ten Black Panthers and two white supporters had been assailed by 150 off-duty police officers and firefighters. This had become typical treatment of the Panthers, as the FBI and police sought to repress the group. Robinson told the National Conference of Christians and Jews of the injustice during a ceremony honoring his human rights service. Before he left to address a closed meeting of the Panthers in Brooklyn, Robinson also related to reporters that in trying to defend themselves, the victims had "every reason to be violent after that kind of violence."[43] Clearly, the Jackie Robinson of 1947, who had followed Branch Rickey's admonition to turn the other cheek in pursuit of long-term goals, had transformed into the "gloves are off" Jackie Robinson who would brook no threats and suffer no fools when it came to race politics.

Nonetheless, Robinson was in a complicated position. Whereas he disagreed with Black Power separatists, he sympathized with African Americans who defended themselves against racist attacks and civil rights violations (Document 37). He was caught between the separatist radicals and the conservatives in the NAACP, from whose board he resigned in 1967 to protest the election of the aging Roy Wilkins as president, whom Robinson deemed to be out of touch with youths. By the late 1960s, Robinson seemed distant from the civil rights movement, even self-righteously so, and unable to bridge its myriad gaps.

He was also torn politically. Although President Lyndon Johnson had launched the War on Poverty and rammed through Congress the Civil Rights Act of 1964 and the Voting Rights Act of 1965, he also had escalated U.S. involvement in the Vietnam War. Arguing that the war diverted resources from domestic programs intended to help the poor and minorities, Martin Luther King Jr. split with Johnson over Vietnam. Robinson worried that King's open break with Johnson would incite charges of Communist subversion against the fracturing civil rights movement, which was already polarized by militants' rejection of King's continued support of civil disobedience. In an April 1967 letter to Johnson, Robinson distanced himself from King and expressed his support of the president, while at the same time expressing concern about increasing involvement in Vietnam (Document 38).

Black rage at oppressive conditions at home erupted in a wave of riots that ignited cities in the North, Midwest, and West every summer from 1965 to 1968. The explosion of the ghettos, along with the assassinations in 1968 of King and civil rights champion and presidential contender Robert F. Kennedy, further depressed Robinson's hopes for remedies to racial discord and economic blight. The Kerner Commission, appointed by Johnson in 1967 to investigate the motivation behind the riots, blamed them on racism. It warned that America was moving toward two societies, separate and unequal, and by the early 1970s, Robinson could not have agreed more (Document 39).

A conservative at heart, Robinson had backed Republican presidential candidates Eisenhower and Nixon, aiming to keep a black presence in the Republican party while also maintaining pressure on northern Democrats regarding civil rights. But he broke with Nixon in the late 1960s over the president's slowdown of desegregation policies. Despite waning health, Robinson remained a tireless protester against segregation and race-based poverty, and he came to believe that the Republicans cared little about minorities. He carried that view into baseball, refusing, for example, to attend an old-timers' game at Yankee Stadium in 1969 because the major leagues fell woefully short of hiring minority executives and managers.

Before the 1968 Summer Olympics in Mexico City, Robinson joined the American Committee on Africa to protest the application for readmission to the Olympics of the racist apartheid regime of South Africa. The committee's threat of a boycott of the games never materialized, as South Africa's bid failed. But in Mexico City, two black U.S. 200-meter sprinters, Tommie Smith and John Carlos (who joined Robinson as signatories to the committee's protest against South Africa), famously accepted their medals by raising clenched fists covered by black gloves, bowing their heads during the national anthem, and wearing badges to express their support of human rights worldwide.[44] Robinson disliked the Black Power movement, but he certainly agreed with the basic complaint about racism. He also increasingly criticized U.S. foreign policy, sounding more and more like Paul Robeson. "I wouldn't fly the flag on the Fourth of July or any other day," he proclaimed in the early 1970s.

"When I see a car with a flag on it, I figure the guy behind the wheel isn't my friend."[45]

ROBINSON'S LEGACY

Jackie Robinson continued the civil rights crusade to the day he died despite personal and family losses. He grew sickly due to heart disease and diabetes, which nearly blinded him in his last year of life. His troubled eldest child, Jackie Jr., who had struggled with drug abuse since being wounded in the Vietnam War, died in a car accident in June 1971. Sixteen months later, in his last national appearance, Robinson was interviewed on television before the second game of the 1972 World Series in Cincinnati. As he gazed at the players and managers assembled from third base to home plate to be honored before the game, he said that he was happy to be there but confessed that he would be "tremendously more pleased and more proud when I look over at that third base coaching line and see a black face managing in baseball."[46] He would not live to see this wish fulfilled, but three years later, in 1975, Frank Robinson (no relation) would achieve the milestone of being the first African American manager, for the Cleveland Indians.

On October 24, 1972, nine days after his World Series remarks, Robinson died of a heart attack at his home in Stamford, Connecticut. He was only fifty-three years old, and the news stunned the nation. More than twenty-five hundred mourners attended Robinson's funeral in New York City, transfixed by the Reverend Jesse Jackson's eulogy (Document 41).[47] Dozens of statements celebrating his life and accomplishments from celebrities and common folk followed in the ensuing days (Documents 42, 43, 44). Born into segregation, Robinson lived to see the legal end to that sordid practice. To honor his achievement, his widow, Rachel, established the Jackie Robinson Foundation in 1973 to provide college scholarships and leadership training opportunities for underserved populations, and she continued to carry on his legacy with the public (Document 45).

In baseball, number 42 is synonymous with the start of racial integration, but not necessarily its success. What about the issue of economic and social opportunity for minorities to fulfill the American dream—the crux of the Robinson experiment? The figures are disheartening. A 1986 survey revealed the continued racial divide. Twice as many black players as white players had lifetime batting averages of .280 or higher, and

40 percent of black pitchers (versus 10 percent of whites) had earned run averages under the respectable mark of 3.00. In other words, black players had to be much better than their white counterparts to earn a spot on major league rosters. These alarming statistics help to explain another one: African Americans comprised less than a tenth of major league players in 2006, while thirty years before, when Robinson passed away, they had represented over a quarter of the big leagues.

The dearth of African American major league players endures. While the 2010 New York Mets (the replacement team, ironically, for Robinson's Brooklyn Dodgers) had eighteen players who represented minorities, seventeen were Latin American and only one was African American. As the major league season opened in April 2012, neither the Chicago White Sox nor the St. Louis Cardinals had an African American player on their roster, and the Chicago Cubs and San Francisco Giants signed but one each.[48] The following year when the 2013 season began, the Giants had no African American players, and the Boston Red Sox, Baltimore Orioles, and Arizona Diamondbacks had only one.[49] So distant seemed the Robinson achievement from the game that Major League Baseball created programs, beginning in 2003, focused on developing the game in urban areas and established the annual Civil Rights Game to recall the struggle in the sport.

Statistics also shed light on the racism faced by other minority groups in baseball, most notably Latin American players, who faced the same sort of exploitation and abuse experienced by Negro Leaguers. For Latin American players, Robinson's feat gave them an upside in terms of opportunity, but also a downside in terms of treatment and meager benefits. Oftentimes, the racism they encountered was more subtle than the taunting faced by American blacks. The flamboyant Puerto Rican hitter Vic Powers was traded by the Yankees in 1954 supposedly for dating a white woman. The brilliant Roberto Clemente, who played for the Pittsburgh Pirates from 1955 until his death in an airplane crash in 1972, was considered by many Latinos to be "our Jackie Robinson," because he showed that a dark-skinned Puerto Rican player could excel in the majors while remaining a gentleman on and off the field. Yet Clemente faced racism from teammates as well as the media.[50]

Nonetheless, the number of Latin American players has grown in baseball, just as the figure for African Americans has withered. By 2013, Latin Americans comprised more than 24 percent of opening day line-ups, up from 13 percent just twenty years before.[51] The remarkably high percentage of Latin Americans in the majors made professional baseball more populated by athletes from that region than any other sport in the

United States. Why is that? To be sure, a business model dominated by major league baseball academies and contracts actually "colonized" Latin American players, in the words of one historian.[52] That is, major league baseball served as an imperial power over Latin American players, who were viewed as subjects to enrich the lords of the sport in the United States. And Latin Americans' success in the majors seemed to push African Americans further from public interest.

Did the pioneering Robinson experiment of 1947 spill over into other realms of the sport, including the top levels? In 1974, some white spectators greeted slugging star Hank Aaron's inspiring quest to surpass Babe Ruth in career home runs with disdain and death threats. Afterward, Aaron long criticized the lack of progress afforded to blacks in baseball's executive levels, and by 1996 only 9 percent of front office personnel in major league baseball were black (Asian and Hispanic employment raised the minority hiring to 18 percent that year). Ten years later, just four of thirty managers were African Americans.[53] Some baseball observers argued that the decline could be attributed to the "fact" that African Americans simply were not capable of high-level management. In 1987, the fortieth anniversary of Robinson's debut, Ted Koppel, host of the popular television show *Nightline*, invited the general manager of the Los Angeles Dodgers, Al Campanis, to discuss the event's impact. He asked the educated, multilingual Campanis why there were not more blacks in decision-making roles in baseball, and Robinson's friend stunningly replied that blacks simply lacked the necessary qualities of leadership. The Dodgers fired Campanis, who faced a backlash of recrimination. Some commentators recalled the words of Jimmy Powers, sports editor of the *New York Daily News*, forty years before when he expressed doubts about Robinson himself. According to Powers, Robinson was "a thousand-to-one shot at best. The Negro players simply don't have the brains or skills."[54] Campanis had merely updated such prejudice to modern times.

The falling number of African Americans in baseball has periodically prompted Americans to debate the opportunities afforded to minorities in sports. Scholars such as Gerald Early have argued that the intimate connections between race and sports are about power. As Early notes, liberals argue with conservatives over the extent to which Robinson changed mainstream America when it came to race, and thus engage in the wider debate over affirmative action and its ability to alter the structure, laws, and ideology of inequality.[55] Sportswriter and columnist William Rhoden has actually accused sports of treating blacks as slaves. The only difference between the contemporary and pre–Civil War plantation eras, asserts Rhoden, is that athletes earn money. Whites are still the owners, and blacks are still the laborers. In multibillion-dollar global sports businesses, Rhoden writes, "African Americans [are] largely shut out—shut out of front office positions, presidencies, vice presidencies, and a wide variety of positions that flow into sports."[56] Ironically, Robinson was complicit in this situation. His appearance as a Brooklyn Dodger was instrumental in the destruction of the Negro Leagues, one group of black-owned enterprises that gave African Americans true power. Thus the complexities of history intruded in his story: The failure of black independence stood side by side with the rival narrative of success in defeating Jim Crow.

Regardless of his faith in America, Jackie Robinson sided with the critics: He certainly agreed that the civil rights crusade had far to go and integration was incomplete. In *I Never Had It Made*, Robinson castigated the white backlash against the civil rights movement (Document 40). He saw that his tremendous victory in 1947 had fallen short of bringing equality, justice, and widespread prosperity for his race, and while he would no doubt see progress today, particularly in the growth of a black middle class, the election of an African American president, and perhaps the coming out of gay athletes, he would lament the lethargy, steps backward, and battles that still characterize the pursuit of civil rights.

When asked the significance of signing the contract with the Montreal Royals in 1945 as the first black man in organized baseball, Robinson replied, "Maybe I'm doing something for my race."[57] Jackie Robinson was both proud of America and critical of it. Joining the Dodgers did not completely transform American race relations, and his life thereafter, though dedicated to civil rights, would not bear out the success he had on the field in integrating baseball. He remained a minority in an America dominated by, and seemingly tailored for, whites. But by running out of the dugout at Ebbets Field on April 15, 1947, he helped to change the social landscape of the United States. He struck a blow against Jim Crow, and his baseball accomplishment would have long-term consequences for the nation.

NOTES

[1] Jules Tygiel, *Baseball's Great Experiment: Jackie Robinson and His Legacy*, exp. ed. (New York: Oxford University Press, 1997), 9.

[2] Ibid., 60.

[3] In 1970, Curt Flood, a center fielder for the St. Louis Cardinals, issued the most serious test of the reserve clause, which had existed in contracts since 1879, by challenging his team's decision to trade him. The U.S. Supreme Court ruled against Flood in 1972, but he paved the way for "free agency," or the ability of a player to leave a team after his

contract has expired and sign with another team. It was no coincidence that Flood, a black man, likened his plight in baseball to slavery by claiming that he was not property to be bought and sold.

[4] Robert Peterson, *Only the Ball Was White: A History of Legendary Black Players and All-Black Professional Teams* (New York: Oxford University Press, 1970), 33.

[5] Rebecca T. Alpert, *Out of Left Field: Jews and Black Baseball* (New York: Oxford University Press, 2011), 9–14.

[6] Samuel O. Regalado, *Viva Baseball! Latin Major Leaguers and Their Special Hunger* (Champaign: University of Illinois Press, 2008); Adrian Burgos, *Playing America's Game: Baseball, Latinos, and the Color Line* (Berkeley: University of California Press, 2007), 88–110.

[7] Bill Wise, *Louis Sockalexis: Native American Baseball Pioneer* (New York: Lee & Low, 2009).

[8] Light-skinned black Cubans, who could "pass" as white, were recruited to play in organized baseball, until they were discovered to be black and summarily dismissed.

[9] Rob Ruck, *Raceball: How the Major Leagues Colonized the Black and Latin Game* (Boston: Beacon Press, 2011), 26–48. Greenlee razed his ballpark in 1938 to pay off debts, although in 1945 he teamed with Branch Rickey to create the black United States Baseball League to break the monopoly of the Negro Leagues on African American players.

[10] Donn Rogosin, *Invisible Men: Life in Baseball's Negro Leagues* (Lincoln: University of Nebraska Press, 1983).

[11] Ibid., 220–21; Neil Lanctot, *Negro League Baseball: The Rise and Ruin of a Black Institution* (Philadelphia: University of Pennsylvania Press, 2008), 320–97.

[12] Peterson, *Only the Ball Was White*, 173.

[13] Lee Finkle, *Forum for Protest: The Black Press during World War II* (Rutherford, N.J.: Fairleigh Dickinson University Press, 1975), 51–52.

[14] Gunnar Myrdal, *An American Dilemma: The Negro Problem and Modern Democracy* (New York: Harper, 1944); Harvard Sitkoff, *A New Deal for Blacks: The Emergence of Civil Rights as a National Issue: The Depression Decade* (New York: Oxford University Press, 1978).

[15] Lewis Erenberg, *The Greatest Fight of Our Generation: Louis vs. Schmeling* (New York: Oxford University Press, 2006), 194.

[16] Quoted in Arnold Rampersad, *Jackie Robinson: A Biography* (New York: Knopf, 1997), 108.

[17] Quoted in Glenn Stout and Dick Johnson, *Jackie Robinson: Between the Baselines* (San Francisco: Woodford Press, 1997), 38.

[18] Tom Gilbert, *Baseball and the Color Line* (New York: Franklin Watts, 1995), 114–16; David K. Wiggins, *Glory Bound: Black Athletes in a White America* (Syracuse: Syracuse University Press, 1997), 84.

[19] Harvey Frommer, *Rickey and Robinson: The Men Who Broke Baseball's Color Barrier* (New York: Macmillan, 1982); Lee Lowenfish, *Branch Rickey: Baseball's Ferocious Gentleman* (Lincoln: University of Nebraska Press, 2007).

[20] Jackie Robinson, *I Never Had It Made: Jackie Robinson, An Autobiography* (New York: HarperCollins, 1995), 33.

[21] Quoted in Clyde Sukeforth, "Oh, They Were a Pair," as told to Donald Honig, in *The Jackie Robinson Reader: Perspectives on an American Hero*, ed. Jules Tygiel (New York: Plume, 1997), 70.

[22] Tygiel, *Baseball's Great Experiment*, 66.

[23] Rampersad, *Jackie Robinson*, 53–54; Jackson Lears, "Providence at Bat," *New Republic*, February 2, 1998, 28.

[24] Jackie Robinson and Wendell Smith, *Jackie Robinson: My Own Story* (New York: Greenberg, 1948), 72.

[25] Tygiel, *Baseball's Great Experiment*, 129.

[26] Quoted in ibid., 76.

[27] Quoted in David Falkner, *Great Time Coming: The Life of Jackie Robinson from Baseball to Birmingham* (New York: Touchstone, 1995), 152.

[28] Red Barber, *1947: When All Hell Broke Loose in Baseball* (Garden City, N.Y.: Doubleday, 1982).

[29] Henry D. Fetter, "Robinson in 1947: Measuring an Uncertain Impact," in *Jackie Robinson: Race, Sports, and the American Dream*, ed. Joseph Dorinson and Joram Warmund (Armonk, N.Y.: M. E. Sharpe, 1998), 183–92. Even a significant rise in black attendance is debatable, despite anecdotal evidence of an influx of African American spectators in every part of the country to see Robinson, because the teams with the greatest attendance gains were in cities with the smallest black populations. Thus it was easy to exaggerate the rise in black fans when so few, if any, had ever been present at a ball game before.

[30] Quoted in Jonathan Eig, *Opening Day: The Story of Jackie Robinson's First Season* (New York: Simon & Schuster Paperbacks, 2007), 95.

[31] Quoted in Rachel Robinson, *Jackie Robinson: An Intimate Portrait* (New York: Harry N. Abrams, 1996), 75.

[32] Quoted in Robinson, *I Never Had It Made*, 58.

[33] Alpert, *Out of Left Field*, 133–92.

[34] Quoted in Tygiel, *Baseball's Great Experiment*, 200.

[35] Quoted in Robinson and Smith, *Jackie Robinson*, 149.

[36] Martin Duberman, *Paul Robeson: A Biography* (New York: New Press, 2005).

[37] For the cold war's effect on civil rights, see Robbie Lieberman and Clarence Lang, eds., *Anticommunism and the African American Freedom Movement: "Another Side of the Story"* (New York: Palgrave Macmillan, 2009).

[38] Duberman, *Paul Robeson*, 361–62; Ronald A. Smith, "The Paul Robeson–Jackie Robinson Saga and a Political Collision," *Journal of Sport History* 6, no. 2 (Summer 1979): 5–27.

[39] Peterson, *Only the Ball Was White*, 204.

[40] Charles K. Ross, *Outside the Lines: African Americans and the Integration of the National Football League* (New York: NYU Press, 2001).

[41] Charles Martin, *Benching Jim Crow: The Rise and Fall of the Color Line in Southern College Sports, 1890–1980* (Champaign: University of Illinois Press, 2010), 204–6.

[42] John R. M. Wilson, *Jackie Robinson and the American Dilemma* (New York: Longman, 2010), 173.

[43] FBI file, UPI press release, September 27, 1968, Federal Bureau of Investigation, *The Vault: Part 5 of 5*, National Archives and Record Service.

[44] Amy Bass, *Not the Triumph but the Struggle: 1968 Olympics and the Making of the Black Athlete* (Minneapolis: University of Minnesota Press, 2004).

[45] Quoted in Robert Elias, *The Empire Strikes Out: How Baseball Sold U.S. Foreign Policy and Promoted the American Way Abroad* (New York: New Press, 2010), 181–82.

[46] Jackie Robinson, "Last Words," www.biography.com/people/jackie-robinson -9460813/videos/jackie-robinson-last-words-2183107128.

[47] Stout and Johnson, *Jackie Robinson*, 193.

[48] Ruck, *Raceball*, 231; Dan McGrath, "Cubs, Sox Not Alone in Their Lack of African-American Players," April 7, 2012.

[49] Nick Cafardo, "MLB Still Lacks Interest from African-Americans," *Boston Globe*, April 13, 2013, www.bostonglobe.com/sports/2013/04/12/mlb-seeks-answer-increasing -african-american-participation-baseball/HfwB6ugfOwQF2WojHZSK7H/story.html.

[50] David Maraniss, *Clemente: The Passion and Grace of Baseball's Last Hero* (New York: Simon & Schuster, 2007), 137–62; Samuel I. Regalado, "Jackie Robinson and the Emancipation of Latin American Baseball Players," in *Jackie Robinson: Race, Sports, and the American Dream*, ed. Joseph Dorinson and Joram Warmund (Armonk, N.Y.: M. E. Sharpe, 1998), 157–65.

[51] Fox News Latino, "Opening Day: Over 28 Percent of MLB Players Are Foreign Born," April 3, 2013, http://latino.foxnews.com/latino/sports/2013/04/03/over-28-percent-players-were-foreign-born-in-mlb-opening-day/.

[52] Ruck, *Raceball*, 195–228.

[53] Richard Lapchick, with Nikki Bowey and Ray Mathew, "The 2008 Racial and Gender Report Card: Major League Baseball," April 15, 2008. www.tidesport.org/RGRC/2008/2008_MLB_RGRC_PR.pdf.

[54] Quoted in Phillip M. Hoose, *Necessities: Racial Barriers in American Sports* (New York: Random House, 1989), xv–xviii.

[55] Gerald Early, *A Level Playing Field: African American Athletes and the Republic of Sports* (Cambridge, Mass.: Harvard University Press, 2011), 193.

[56] William C. Rhoden, *$40 Million Slaves: The Rise, Fall, and Redemption of the Black Athlete* (New York: Crown, 2006), 125.

[57] Quoted in Rick Swaine, *The Black Stars Who Made Baseball Whole: The Jackie Robinson Generation in the Major Leagues, 1947–1959* (Jefferson City, N.C.: MacFarland, 2006), 23.

PART TWO

The Documents

1

Segregation and Steps to Integration

1

DAILY WORKER

A Fan Wants Negro Stars

February 14, 1937

*The U.S. Communist party, which led the charge for the integration
of professional baseball, began in 1924 to publish the* Daily Worker, *a
newspaper based in New York City. At its peak, the* Daily Worker *had
a circulation of thirty-five thousand subscribers. It consistently toed the
Stalinist line, even upholding the infamous purge trials of the 1930s that
led to the death and imprisonment of thousands of people in the Soviet
Union. The* Daily Worker *also equated communism with American
ideals of liberty and social justice as it expanded its coverage into entertainment and the arts. In 1935, the newspaper established a sports
section, publicizing, in particular, racial discrimination in professional
sports. This letter from a reader typifies the strident call to end Jim Crow
in baseball.*

As a former minor league player, with eleven seasons with the Rochester club and as baseball coach at James Monroe and Morris High School
for several years, I feel competent to speak on baseball in relation to
Negro players and labor sports.

During the seasons that I was with the Bronx Giants, a Class A semi-
pro nine, I played against many colored teams. In my opinion, there
has never been a Negro tosser [pitcher] who could zip them over like

From "A Fan Wants Negro Stars," *Daily Worker*, February 14, 1937, 14.

"Cannon Ball" Joe Williams, with all due respect to Satchel Paige. Williams was with the Lincoln Giants.[1] His fastball was every bit as good as Walter Johnson's[2] and his curves [curveballs] broke as though propelled by a machine. Smart and with a change of pace,[3] Cannon Ball Joe would have been one of the greatest pitchers of our time in the majors. . . .

The reasons given by the magnates [major league team owners] for discriminating against these Negro players are too ridiculous and pussyfooting to stand up against the cold light of reason. The fans are demanding that the bars be let down and that day would be hastened if exhibition games could be arranged between the major clubs and such nines as the Lincoln Giants, Harrisburg Giants, Homestead Grays, and Pittsburgh Crawfords, not to mention many other great Negro teams.

To a great extent, the same discrimination is practiced against Jewish players. In the old days, a Jewish player had to change his name to get into the big-time leagues. Today, although there are a few Jewish stars, the best of whom is Hank Greenberg,[4] whom I coached at Monroe, the odds are against a Jewish player getting an honest trial.

The way has been shown by the organization of the Trade Union Sports Federation. Only through the intensive and consistent building of Labor Sports will we manage to destroy these reactionary and chauvinistic characteristics of major baseball and give the game back to the boys who play it;—from the shops, the farms, the mines, offices, and the schools.

Clean up baseball by building a powerful labor sports organization!

---

[1] A Negro League team based in New York City.

[2] The preeminent fastball pitcher for the Washington Senators from 1907 to 1927, known as "the Big Train" for his sheer power and velocity.

[3] Also known as an off-speed pitch, in which the ball travels much more slowly to the plate than a fastball and tricks the batter into swinging early.

[4] The preeminent power hitter (slugger) of the 1930s, first baseman Greenberg played for the Detroit Tigers.

2

WESTBROOK PEGLER

Baseball Treats Negroes as Hitler Does Jews

Pittsburgh Press, *August 4, 1938*

The iconoclastic Pulitzer Prize–winning journalist Westbrook Pegler was a thorn to liberals and conservatives alike, including President Franklin D. Roosevelt, labor unions, and people and organizations he deemed to have fascist qualities. The youngest American war correspondent during World War I and a sportswriter after the war, Pegler joined the Scripps Howard newspaper syndicate in 1933. By the 1940s, his columns were run in 174 newspapers and reached an estimated ten million readers. His column Fair Enough, from which this excerpt is taken, was published throughout the United States. The Pittsburgh Press, *established in 1884, was one of the city's two major newspapers.*

New York—Jake Powell, a part-time outfielder for the New York Yankees, is riding the pine[1] for 10 days for blurting out in an impromptu broadcast on the field in Chicago that he spent his winters doing police work and that his specialty was hitting Negroes over the head with his club.

Judge Landis,[2] who tried the case and imposed the penalty, thus would placate the Negro clientele of a business which trades under the name of the national game, but always has treated the Negroes as Adolf Hitler treats the Jews.

If all American employers did the same the entire Negro population of this country would starve, become public charges or go back to slavery. So Powell was only giving expression in crude, brief wordage to

---

[1] Baseball jargon for sitting on the bench.
[2] Commissioner of Baseball Kenesaw Mountain Landis, who served as a judge on the U.S. District Court for the Northern District of Illinois from 1905 to 1922 and then as commissioner until he died, in 1944. As commissioner, he repeatedly refused either to speak about integration or to change the unwritten agreement by the owners to preserve segregation.

From Westbrook Pegler, "Baseball Treats Negroes as Hitler Does Jews, Pegler Says," Fair Enough, *Pittsburgh Press*, August 4, 1938, 17.

the unspoken but inflexible policy of the organized baseball industry. Moreover his remark was thoughtless and probably untrue, whereas the men who employ him and Judge Landis have given solemn study to the problem and confirmed their decision by their conduct.

Ban on Negros

Thus no Negro has ever been permitted to play ball or even to try out for a job in the organized industry, and Babe Ruth,[3] were he a Negro, would not have risen above the rank and pay of the leaky-roof leagues in which Negroes operate as semi-pros.

In the semi-pro business, however, for more than a quarter of a century, white men have played on good terms against teams of Negroes. The white men have included major leaguers come down in the world, unemployed minor leaguers, part-time mediocrities playing for a little extra cash and love of the game and some current major league players out barnstorming[4] after their work was done. . . .

Practical Difficulties

Many of the white players are Southern men who would object to Negroes, and the national organization of baseball is such that men must be farmed out to minor leagues playing in Southern cities where a Negro would be unwelcome on the field in white company. These are practical difficulties which the magnates [owners] have had to consider, and it is no fault of theirs that the prejudice exists.

However, they have been content to respect the prejudice and have never done anything to soften it up, even in Northern cities where public opinion would have approved the granting of an opportunity to a pioneer Negro major or minor leaguer. By the time half a dozen Negroes had been given a chance, some to fail on their merits, no doubt, the novelty would wear off, and organized baseball, in certain areas, at least, would be free of discrimination on racial grounds.

From the standpoint of the customers there would be no risk at all north of the [Mason-Dixon] line, for they have seen and cheered many Negro fighters and a few football players in open competition and

---

[3] George Herman "Babe" Ruth, who retired from the New York Yankees in 1936 as the most popular player of his era.

[4] Touring the country, playing baseball exhibitions.

bodily contact with white men. And if there is danger in Harlem[5] it would be diminished, not aggravated, by a decision to permit Negro players to make good or fail according to their skill.

Easy to Rage

It is easy to rage at the major leagues and denounce the magnates for bowing to a prejudice that was none of their doing, but if they were to open up the game completely to Negro players overnight, they would bring on disorder and defeat the reform. Consistently they would have to impose Negro recruits and reserve players on Southern communities where they operate, and the South just wouldn't agree.

But the baseball business does nothing at all about this discrimination, and Jake Powell can argue plausibly that he got his cue from the very men whose hired disciplinarian has benched him for an idle remark.

The Yankees or one of the Chicago teams could easily try the experiment of using a star Negro player from one of the [Negro Leagues] clubs. The customers would suffer no shock, and the Southern white boys would find after a few games that it didn't hurt them much after all.

---

[5] A section of New York City and home to a large black community.

3

JACKIE ROBINSON

Letter to Assistant Secretary of War Truman K. Gibson

July 16, 1944

Lieutenant Jackie Robinson was court-martialed for supposed insults to a white bus driver and to other officers while stationed at Fort Hood, Texas. In this letter, written from the U.S. Army's neighboring McCloskey General Hospital in Temple, where he was recuperating from an injury, he tries to explain the incident. Truman K. Gibson Jr., an African American serving as the secretary of war's civilian aide, who had befriended Robinson, passed this letter up the chain of command. Next to the address line, Gibson scribbled, "This man is the well-known athlete. He will write you. Follow the case carefully." Robinson was honorably discharged from the Army.

Truman K. Gibson
Ass't to Sec of War
Washington D.C.

16 JULY 44

Sir:

I am sorry to bother you again but under the circumstances there seems to be no alternative.

On or about the 7th of July I was at Camp Hood, Texas visiting the colored officers club and upon leaving I took a shuttle bus from the club to the central station. As I moved to the rear I noticed one of the officer's wife and sat down beside her. The lady is very fair and to many people looks to be white. It is evident the driver seemed to resent my talking to her and told me to move to the rear. He didn't ask the lady to move so I refused. When I did he threatened to make trouble for me when we reached the bus station. Upon reaching the bus station a white lady tells

Jackie Robinson to Truman K. Gibson, letter, July 16, 1944, in John Vernon, "Jim Crow, Meet Lieutenant Robinson: A 1944 Court-Martial," Records of the Office of the Secretary of War, RG 107, National Archives, Washington, D.C.

me that she is going to pr[off]er charges against me. She said she heard the driver tell me to move to the rear. I told her I didn't care if she pr[off]ered charges against me and she went away angry. That is the last that was said to the lady and the next thing I hear is I've cursed a white lady out. I feel now that I should have but I have never cursed one out and I certainly didn't start with her.

I need a little advice. I want to know just how far I should go with the case. What I mean is should I appeal to the NAACP and the Negro Press? I don't want any unfavorable publicity for myself or the Army but I believe in fair play and I feel I have to let someone in on the case. If I write the NAACP I hope to get statements from all the witnesses because a broad minded person can see how the people framed me.

You can see sir that I need your advice. I don't care what the outcome of the trial is because I know I am being framed and the charges aren't too bad. I would like to get your advice about the publicity. I have a lot of good publicity out and I feel I have numerous friends on the press but I first want to hear from you before I do any thing I will be sorry for later on.

Sir as I said I don't mind trouble but I do believe in fair play and justice. I feel that I'm being taken in this case and I will tell people about it unless the trial is fair. Let me hear from you so I will know what steps to take.

LT. JACK ROBINSON

War 11 B

McClosk[e]y Gen. Hosp.

Temple Texas

4

Recommended Report for the Mayor's Committee on Baseball

September 28, 1945

New York City mayor Fiorello La Guardia convened the Committee on Baseball in August 1944 to push for integration. The group's origins are hazy. Some hold that it was a product of pressure from black sportswriter Sam Lacy on New York Yankees president and general manager Larry MacPhail and Dodgers chief executive Branch Rickey. Others claim that the committee was La Guardia's own idea. By the time the final report was issued, in November 1945, Rickey and MacPhail had resigned from the committee—the former to divorce himself from any hint of politicization and the latter out of protest. The views of MacPhail—who despised Rickey and tried to undermine him at every turn, including on the race question—are also a bit of a mystery; like all major league baseball executives except Rickey, he would vote against integration in 1947. Ten prominent figures, eight white and two black, made up the committee: chairman John Johnson, a black clergyman; MacPhail; Rickey; former New York State Supreme Court justice Jeremiah Mahoney (who had led the effort to boycott Hitler's 1936 Olympic Games due to Nazi racial policies); former presiding justice of the Appellate Division in Brooklyn, Edward Lazansky; New York State Supreme Court justice Charles S. Colden of Queens, New York; Daniel Higgins of the New York City Board of Education; professor of economics Robert M. Haig of Columbia University; New York Times *sports columnist Arthur Daley, the first reporter sent overseas by any U.S. newspaper on a sports assignment (to the 1936 Olympics); and famed former tap dancer Bill Robinson, the first black man to appear on film with a white female (in* The Little Colonel *[1935], starring Shirley Temple).*

We, your Committee on Baseball, wish to submit the following report:

We have examined the problem of integration of Negroes in major league baseball and have attempted to survey the types of problems

From "Recommended Report for the Mayor's Committee on Baseball," folder 13, box 2, Jules Tygiel Papers, A. Bartlett Giamatti Research Library, National Baseball Hall of Fame and Museum, Cooperstown, N.Y.

relating thereto. We feel that in order to present the problem in its real light, it is necessary to review briefly the major problems of the profession as they relate to Negroes as a minority. . . .

The Equity of Negro Baseball

The Committee could not overlook the equity of the vested interests which Negroes have in their own leagues. It is estimated that they do a $2,000,000 a year business and the New York Yankee management point[s] out that last year, Negro teams paid $100,000 in rentals and concessions for their four parks in New York, Kansas City, Newark, and Norfolk.

These rights cannot be overlooked and yet any major social reform must inevitably run up against such vested interests. It has been pointed out that organized Negro baseball would not have been necessary had Negroes been integrated into the system the same as other minority groups.

Yet, many familiar with Negro baseball feel that Negro teams meet a need among Negroes which would not be met by their integration into the profession. The Negro baseball game is much more a gala community affair in which there is a considerable amount of visiting, much more of a holiday spirit, and a release that comes from participating in an All-Negro affair which would not be possible otherwise.

It has been pointed out by those in the profession that the Negro players are under contract or reservation to club[s] in Negro leagues and that this contractual relationship could not be violated and that the signing of the better Negro players in the major leagues would destroy the interest of Negro teams. . . .

Qualification of Negro Players for Big League Participation

. . . Not having had the opportunity to participate in organized baseball and compete against whites under the same standards, it is difficult even for the scouts, who are the experts, to determine whether the players are good "baseball" players or simply good "Negro" baseball players.

Not only must skill in the game be taken into account but it is also necessary to make allowances for temperament. Obviously, any Negro players going into major league baseball will be on the spot and will eventually have to carry the weight of their race on their shoulders as well as the weight of their own personal responsibility. This is a terrific burden for any man and should not be necessary but unfortunately is at the present time. Furthermore, it is necessary for such players to have the experience of competing with whites and this requires experience in minor leagues.

The Yankee management contend[s] that the average amount of time spent in the minor leagues by the players on their roster is seven years, and that the average of the players in major league baseball as a whole is around three years.

This factor cannot be overlooked in appraising the potentialities of Negroes is this sport. It would be relatively easy for any club to set back the cause of race relations for a long time to come by simply employing a mediocre Negro player and allowing him to be "butchered" in major league competition. That, we must be certain does not happen and the only way to keep it from happening will be to provide opportunities for Negroes to perform against whites and with whites in integrated minor league experience.

Difficulties of Integration

The Committee has not overlooked the difficulties involved in the integration of Negro players:

1. An analysis of the birthplace of the players in major league baseball reveals the fact that approximately 35% come from states where there is traditional prejudice against Negroes.

This creates a considerable difficulty in integrating Negroes into the profession. For after all, there is scarcely a field of competition in which tempers are so easily frayed as that of baseball. It is not an uncommon occurrence under the strictest discipline to have two or three fights per season among major league players at the present. The possibilities of this sort of incident, where a Negro player slides into second base and spikes a Southern white boy or vice versa is, of course, a problem to take into account.

2. The problem of spring training is another difficulty to be overcome. Most training is done either in Florida or Cuba. Florida is traditional in its prejudice and, no doubt, if a Negro player accompanied a team to the swanky hotels, he would not be accommodated. This, the Negro player must take into account and must make allowances for in facing his responsibility.

It is not at all certain that the teams would be welcome at the better hotels in border state cities of Washington, D.C., Cincinnati, and St. Louis where the teams are usually accommodated, if they carried on their roster Negro players. If they were not, the Negro would have to understand and make his adjustments to it.

3. Team-work. After all, baseball involves the highest degree of cooperative team performance. The question is raised as to whether or not this could be secured and morale could be maintained if a Negro were a member of the team.

However, the war experience has shown that where management took a firm stand and went about a process of integration correctly, very few problems resulted. In New York City, in all the ways in which Negroes were integrated into industry and many of them worked alongside whites with Southern background, not a single hate strike was certified to the War Labor Board.[1]

It would be a sad commentary, both on the part of management and the teams if organized baseball, which allegedly holds to the highest ideals of sportsmanship of any sport in the country, cannot approximate this performance of labor.

4. Difficulty of attracting the new players. The leadership in the baseball profession has experienced some concern regarding the ability to attract new players. Southern boys, who are being sought both by teams who practice prejudice and those which do not practice discrimination, might prefer to go with the Jim Crow team than the other.

This consideration is no doubt a valid one. On the other hand, the three teams in New York City are in a strategic position to offer other inducements which more than cancel such difficulties. One of these is the greater amount of salary which is paid. Two teams in New York City passed the million mark in gate receipts and the third would have, had not a phenomenal long run of week-end games been rained out. Furthermore, so much of the national publicity centers around the teams in New York City, that the prestige of playing on these teams, in our opinion, more than cancels out the difficulties involved.

5. The next of these difficulties is that of reprisals on the part of other clubs of the baseball leagues.

These organizations will have to remember that the three teams in New York City are "on the spot." First, because of the legislation[2] and second because of the fact that these clubs will have a difficult time maintaining amicable public relations unless they can conform to public opinion.

It is also doubtful inasmuch as all the major league teams are outside of the Southern part of the United States, if any of these teams can long

---

[1] A government body that arbitrated labor–management disputes to prevent work stoppages that would undermine the war effort.

[2] In 1944, the New York State legislature made it illegal to discriminate in employment on the basis of race.

maintain their present policies of racial segregation. If sportsmanship is to be maintained in the great American tradition, it is inevitable that this bottleneck, whereby 10% of the population of the United States are forbidden the right of competition, must go. . . .

Recommendations

After careful consideration of these problems, the Committee wishes to make the following recommendations:

1. That Organized Baseball undertake in their proposed postwar expansion, the organization of Southern communities of B, C, and/or D minor leagues[3] among Negroes as well as among whites and that Northern communities adopt immediately a principle of complete integration of Negroes as well as other minorities at the levels at which their abilities qualify them.

This should be no handicap in the major portion of the United States and baseball cannot neglect its responsibility for this development.

2. That the Negro baseball leagues be admitted into the field of organized baseball and come under the baseball commissioner's jurisdiction and play under the same standards as those developed in the remainder of the baseball field and that their leagues be classified at whatever level their quality of performance allows, whether it be AA or D.

3. Furthermore, we recommend that these Negro leagues, which will no doubt continue to service a unique demand in the Negro community, be given special consideration by the major league clubs operating in the largest cities both in regard to cooperation in scheduling of games and with regard to rentals and concessions in their stadia.

There is much criticism of the exploitation of the Negro teams by the concessionaries and managers of parks and furthermore, we recommend that contractual relations be established with these clubs on a basis comparable to that arranged between clubs within the major and minor leagues.

If it is profitable for the "Yankees" to own a white club in Newark, it should be likewise profitable for them to own a Negro club in New York City or elsewhere or, failing of this relationship, certainly con-

---

[3] These leagues ranked below "Triple-A," the designation created in 1946 for the minor league level just below the major leagues. In 1946, Robinson played in the Triple-A International League. Below this were "Double-A," and "Single-A" leagues. The "D" leagues are today's junior (rookie) leagues, and the "B" and "C" leagues disappeared in the 1950s due to an economic downturn in the minors as a whole.

tractual agreements could be developed as those existing between the "Dodgers" and St. Paul, Mobile, Burlington, and Zanesville.

In this fashion, the contractual relationships between club managers of Negroes and major league teams could be adequately handled.

4. We recommend that simultaneously with, but not dependent upon, this organizational set up, the New York clubs integrate Negroes at whatever level their abilities merit both in major league clubs and in farm systems—keeping in mind the recommendations made in #1 above.

Certainly, in "Dodger," "Yankee," and "Giant" farms in the International League, Negro players who might qualify for experience in this league could be used without difficulty.

The same would perhaps be true with any clubs of the Pacific Coast and no doubt with the major clubs of the American Association except Louisville.[4]

Once this set up is achieved, there should be no difficulty of promotion of Negroes within the system. Any antipathies existing between groups would soon be overcome for organized baseball the United States over, because of the fact that Southern white players, in acquiring their experience in the minor leagues, would have included in that experience that of playing with and against Negro players.

In Conclusion

There was never a more propitious moment than the present, when we are just concluding a terrible World War to suppress the theory of racial superiority, to put our house in order.

The Committee is not asking that major league baseball inject the race issue to the extent of lowering its standards. No one demands that Negroes be integrated at levels above their abilities.

This would be the last desire of any member of this Committee. The Committee does believe that organized baseball owes the same responsibility to the community as does every other sport, business, or industry to make sure that this vicious pattern of race segregation is eliminated.

---

[4] Both the Pacific Coast League and the American Association were elevated to the Triple-A level in 1946. The reference to the Louisville Colonels reveals worries about segregation in the city.

5

JACKIE ROBINSON AND WENDELL SMITH

Interview with Branch Rickey

1948

Branch Rickey claimed that he had sent out careful feelers in his pro-
longed search for the most suitable African American player to break
the color barrier in major league baseball. That was not entirely true.
Although he dispatched scouts across the country to observe Negro League
players, he relied on the efforts of Clyde Sukeforth, who had joined the
Dodgers' coaching staff in 1943. The black press had already identified
Jackie Robinson as a candidate, and Sukeforth followed the trail. Rob-
inson arrived in New York for his interview with Rickey (Sukeforth was
the only other person present) under the mistaken impression that Rickey
was going to sign him to a contract with the Brooklyn Brown Dodgers of
the all-black United States League. Rickey both bantered with and grilled
Robinson, focusing on character over ball-playing skills. This account
comes from Robinson's first memoir, written with Wendell Smith. Lyrical
if often sarcastic and long-winded, Smith began his journalistic career
with the Pittsburgh Courier *in 1937 and covered the Negro Leagues as*
the newspaper's sports editor. A former ballplayer, he was a leading figure
among the black press in support of integration and a key source of infor-
mation for Rickey, who placed Smith on his payroll. Smith posthumously
entered the National Baseball Hall of Fame in 1994.

When I walked into his office that bright August morning, Mr. Rickey was sitting behind his big desk. He smiled broadly and his deep-set eyes sparkled under his bushy eyebrows. "Come in, come in," he said hospitably. "I'm very glad to see you. Clyde Sukeforth tells me you're quite a ball player, Jackie."

I guess I was a little awkward. I didn't want to appear too modest, and yet I didn't want to convey the impression that I had a big head. Sukeforth, standing beside me, rose to the occasion.

From Jackie Robinson and Wendell Smith, *Jackie Robinson: My Own Story* (New York: Greenberg, 1948), 21–23.

"He's the Brooklyn type of player," Sukey said in that soft, accurate voice of his. "The boy can run like blazes and looks like he might be a pretty fair country [powerful] hitter."

Mr. Rickey nodded approvingly. He picked up a tattered stub that had once been a reasonable facsimile of a cigar. He looked at me like a pawn broker examining some trinket brought in by an unfamiliar customer. His piercing eyes roamed over me with such meticulous care, I felt almost naked.

It was a little embarrassing. I shifted uneasily and for want of something to do jammed my hand down in my coat pocket. I don't know what I expected to find there, but I guess I was searching for something to hold on to. Perhaps I'd find a pencil, or maybe some coins. I felt I needed something in my hands right then, something firm and strong.

"Do you drink?" Mr. Rickey suddenly asked.

"No, sir," I said rather proudly.

"That's fine," he said, relaxing in his chair. "Sit down, sit down. We have a lot to talk about." Sukey and I reacted to the order as though it had been given by a five-star general.

"Do you know why you are here, Jackie?" he asked.

I said all I knew was that Sukeforth had told me he had instructions to bring me to Brooklyn.

"Well," Mr. Rickey said slowly and carefully. "I am interested in bringing you into the Brooklyn organization. I have never seen you play, but my scouts have. If Sukeforth says you're a good ball player, I'll take his word for it. He's been around and knows a prospect when he sees one. He thinks, as do some of my other men, you could make good on one of our top farm clubs [minor league teams]."

Needless to say, I was excited. The thought of playing on a farm club of a major league team sent little electric shocks up and down my spine. Here was my chance—the chance to be affiliated with a big league team. Even if I weren't good enough, I could someday tell my grandchildren that I had at least had the opportunity.

Then Mr. Rickey told me I would have to stand a lot of gaff without losing my temper or making a scene. He even acted out several situations I'd be likely to face, and then asked how I would meet each one of them. I wasn't too happy over the prospect he foresaw, but I knew, too, that I was pretty sure to run into some name-calling, some insults, some Jim Crow.

I told him I felt pretty sure I would stay out of rhubarbs [fights] on the field and trouble of any sort away from it, but that I couldn't become an obsequious, cringing fellow. Among other things, I couldn't play hard, aggressive ball if I were that sort of man.

Mr. Rickey seemed satisfied because he changed the subject: "I haven't made up my mind which farm club we'll put you on," Mr. Rickey continued, "but whatever it is, I want you to understand one thing: there will be no limitations as to how far you can go. We will not consider you in any way different from the rest of the players we have in this organization. You are simply another ball player trying to make the grade. If you are good enough, you'll wind up on top. If you aren't, you'll be sent down to another league or released outright."

You could have knocked me over with a feather! Had my ears betrayed me? Could I be wide awake and of sound mind? Yes, as he continued to talk, I realized that he was serious and that I was not dreaming.

6

CHICAGO DAILY TRIBUNE

Baseball Gives Contract to First Negro Player

October 25, 1945

The pressure to integrate major league baseball grew stronger during World War II, as African Americans campaigned for a "double victory" over racism abroad and at home. In baseball, Rickey sought to preempt the La Guardia committee report that advocated integration in baseball (Document 4), which he feared would mire the Dodgers in civil rights issues and detract from his own integration plan for baseball. Thus he went public with his plans to sign a black player to a contract in organized baseball. This article from the Chicago Daily Tribune, *a news outlet that had been historically hostile to civil rights, typifies the tepid treatment of the issue by big-city newspapers.*

Montreal, Que., Oct. 23—The first Negro Player ever to be admitted to organized baseball was signed tonight by the Brooklyn Dodgers for their International league farm club, the Montreal Royals.

From "Baseball Gives Contract to First Negro Player," *Chicago Daily Tribune*, October 25, 1945, 1.

Jackie Robinson, one time University of California at Los Angeles half back and recent shortstop of the Kansas City Negro Monarchs, put his signature on a contract calling not only for a player's salary but also a bonus.

Robinson, product of a three-year search and $25,000 hunt for Negro diamond talent by Branch Rickey, president of the Dodgers, signed up after a conference with Hector Racine and Lt. Col. Romeo Gauvreau, Royals' president and vice president respectively, and Branch Rickey Jr., who heads the Brooklyn farm system.

"Mr. Racine and my father," said the young Rickey in making the announcement, "will undoubtedly be severely criticized in some sections of the United States where racial prejudice is rampant. They are not inviting trouble, but they won't avoid it if it comes. Jack Robinson is a fine type of young man, intelligent and college bred, and I think he can take it, too."

"I can't begin to tell you how happy I am that I am the first member of my race in organized ball," declared Robinson, a 6 foot 190 pounder. "I realize how much it means to me, to my race, and to baseball. I can only say I'll do my very best to come through in every manner." . . .

"It may cost the Brooklyn organization a number of ball players," [Branch Rickey] said. "Some of them, particularly if they come from certain sections of the south, will steer away from a club with colored players on its roster. Some players now with us may even quit. But they'll be back in baseball after they work a year or two in a cotton mill."

7

NEW YORK TIMES

Club Heads Give Views

October 24, 1945

Few executives in organized baseball spoke about integration, and no owner but Branch Rickey supported the elevation of blacks. With the help of Commissioner Albert Benjamin "Happy" Chandler, a southerner whom the owners had expected to be a segregationist, Rickey cautiously circumvented fellow executives and presented them, eventually, with a fait accompli. The owners, managers, and other leaders expressed a range of opinions about Robinson's contract, as this article from the New York Times *reveals.*

Comments on the signing of Jack Robinson, as gathered by the Associated Press, follow:

Horace Stoneham, President of the [New York] Giants—"That's really a fine way to start the program. We will scout the Negro leagues next year, looking for younger prospects. However, the primary responsibility we have is finding places for our returning Service men, numbering into the hundreds, and only if they prove incapable will new players be placed on our clubs."

Clark Griffith, President of the [Washington] Senators—"The only question that occurs to me is whether organized ball has the right to sign a player from the Negro league. That is a well-established league and organized baseball shouldn't take their players. The Negro league is entitled to full recognition as a full-fledged baseball organization."

William E. Benswanger, President of the [Pittsburgh] Pirates—"It is an affair of the Brooklyn and Montreal clubs whom they may sign, whether white or colored."

Frank Shaughnessy, President of the International League—"There's no rule in baseball that says a Negro can't play with a club in organized ball. As long as any fellow's the right type and can make good and can get along with other players, he can play ball. I don't think that much

---

From "Club Heads Give Views," *New York Times*, October 24, 1945, 17.

prejudice exists any longer. I believe such things are more political than social now. . . . There should be no ban on Negro participation in any sport anywhere. The signing of any player is up to the particular club involved. If he makes good and is the right type, he plays."

Joseph Brown, Secretary of the Buffalo Bisons[1] — "Very surprising, it's hard to believe. I can't understand it."

Eddie Collins, general manager of the [Boston] Red Sox — "Robinson worked out for us last spring. Very few players can step into the majors from college or sandlot[2] baseball. Of course, they always have a chance to prove themselves in the minors. More power to Robinson if he can make the grade."

[1] An International League team affiliated with the Detroit Tigers.
[2] Informal or semiprofessional baseball, or perhaps a denigrating reference to the Negro Leagues.

8

NEW YORK AMSTERDAM NEWS

A Crack in Baseball Jim Crow

November 3, 1945

Founded in 1909, the New York Amsterdam News *was one of the four most widely circulated African American newspapers in the United States, alongside the* Pittsburgh Courier, *the* Chicago Defender, *and the* Afro-American. *The brainchild of businessman James Anderson, who named it after the street on which he lived, the* Amsterdam News *was based in Harlem. In the 1940s, its audience climbed above 100,000 readers in the New York area. The newspaper ran articles by leading civil rights and political figures in the black community, such as W. E. B. Du Bois and Roy Wilkins, who were in the forefront of the civil rights movement. In this editorial, it links the Dodgers' signing of Robinson to other assaults on Jim Crow.*

"A Crack in Baseball Jim Crow," *New York Amsterdam News*, November 3, 1945, 12.

The signing of Jackie Robinson by the Brooklyn Dodgers for their Montreal farm team came at a very good time. We needed something to offset the growing depression of triumphant racialism.

This is the sum of their piling on:

Rapidly growing mass unemployment of Negroes; revival of the Ku Klux Klan in Atlanta, Ga.; ascendancy of jim-crowism in Washington, D.C.; rampant imperialism in Indonesia, India, and Africa; twisted bitterness of returned Negro soldiers; frustrated resentment of parents at inadequate schools and arrogant race-hate strikes; skyrocketing prices and shrinking income.

The cracking of baseball jim-crow, one of the most flagrant anti-Negro institutions, is just the drop of water in the drought that keeps faith alive in American institutions.

It is descriptive of the method of American progress that shades and shadows of opinion had some part in the final triumph of justice over bigotry. And it is the victory of a sense of justice in the mind and heart of Branch Rickey, Dodger president.

The beginning has been made. The weight of demonstration rests on the athletic shoulders of Jackie Robinson.

He has a doubly difficult job to do.

It is a major victory to reach the peak of the heap in any competitive field. There are many youths of high ambition and considerable personal equipment who aspire to be "big league" in baseball, only to eat out their hearts in frustration and disappointment. But, in addition, on Jackie Robinson is laid the extra weight of being "The First Negro."

This is a psychological hazard that should not be minimized.

The weight of knowing how much race pride and how much the future of youngsters hangs in the balance can be an oppressive although challenging load.

And in addition to the normal worries of a "rookie," Robinson must face additional problems of where to eat, sleep, or live. Also, his ability to play ball will always have a shadow of super-criticism hanging over it, to magnify his mistakes and to distort every incident.

Yet this is the way baseball jim-crow will be killed. After so much controversy and verbiage, the clear answer will come when the Dodgers are trailing in the last inning and Jackie Robinson poles one "over the fence" [hits a home run], to bring the home team out of a hole and victory to Montreal, and incidentally, "Brooklyn."

As in all competitive fields, where merit has a chance to show, baseball, along with boxing and track, will discover the best man will always win the plaudits of the great American audience. The bulk of American people are willing to give homage and praise to accomplishment—without looking for a color label.

This is the spirit of America.

This spirit must and will win in the end.

It now rests with Jackie Robinson to take the ball. He has the best wishes and support of everybody in the community interested in justice and clean American sports and democracy.

9

JACKIE ROBINSON AND WENDELL SMITH

Facing Jim Crow

1948

In Deland, Florida, the Montreal Royals faced a minor league team from Indianapolis during one of their 1946 spring training exhibitions. Rumors circulated that officials would bar Robinson from the field. Clay Hopper, the manager of the Royals, who had initially opposed Jackie's signing, was appalled by the actions of his fellow white southerners. Johnny Wright, the Negro Leaguer who accompanied Robinson in Florida, was also signed by Montreal as a possible replacement for Robinson. He spent a season in the International League, in 1946, and was then demoted back to the Negro Leagues. Following is Robinson's account of his reception in Deland, from his first memoir, written with black journalist Wendell Smith (see Document 5).

We were the visiting team and consequently I batted first. I was up second and got a base hit. I stole second and the next hitter, Tom Tatum, singled to left center. I took off for third base and [Clay] Hopper, who was in the coaching box, waved me on home. I rounded the bag under full steam and headed for the plate. I knew it was going to be close and that I'd have to slide to make it. I took a big breath and left my

From Jackie Robinson and Wendell Smith, *Jackie Robinson: My Own Story* (New York: Greenberg, 1948), 80, 97–98.

feet, sliding across just ahead of the throw. The stands were cheering and I felt good. We were one run ahead and it was still the first inning. But before I could get up and head for the bench, a strong firm hand appeared through the cloud of dust I had raised and grasped me by the collar. At first, I thought the next batter on my team was trying to help me up, and I was about to thank him. But just then, the dust cleared away and I recognized the standard uniform of the Law.

"Now you git off'n this heah field right now," he drawled. "Eff'n ya don't, ah'm puttin' ya' in the jail house right now. So hep me eff ah don't!"

At first, I was tempted to laugh, but I could see he was dead serious. I suddenly saw myself behind bars wearing a baseball uniform. . . . By this time the crowd in the stands was on its feet. The Indianapolis ball players didn't move. They just stayed at their positions, waiting to see what was going to happen. The policeman finally released his death-grip on my collar and I sauntered toward the bench. Hopper, obviously flustered, made a belated and reluctant appearance in the dugout. "What's wrong?" he asked in a voice as typically Southern as the policeman's. "He didn't do anything wrong, did he?"

"Yes, he did," the cop snapped back.

"What?" Hopper asked meekly.

" We told y'all to leave them Nigra players home," said Deland's legal guardian. "We ain't having Nigras and white boys playing on the same field in this town. It's agin the law and ah'm heah to tell ya."

Hopper turned to see if I had gone to the dressing room. I hadn't. I was sitting on the bench with the rest of the team, watching the show. The cop was looking at me, too. He had a scowl on his sun-tanned countenance; certainly, he wasn't in a jovial mood.

"Y'all ain't up-states now," the policeman informed Hopper. "Ya can't come down heah and change our way of livin'. They's a law says Nigras and whites cain't be togetha. They cain't sit togetha; and ya' know damn well they cain't git married togetha!"

I felt sorry for Hopper. He didn't know what to do. He knew he had to do what the cop said, but he didn't want to have to tell me to leave the game. I knew then he was beginning to like me.

"Git him off'en thet there bench," the cop demanded, waving his menacing-looking club. "He cain't set there. They's white boys a-setin' there. Thet's agin the law, too. They cain't sit togetha on no baseball benches, either."

By now the crowd was shouting for the game to continue. The players were getting restless and so was the cop. In order to relieve Hopper the embarrassment of having to tell me to leave, I decided to do it voluntarily.

Hopper started walking toward the bench. I guess he had decided he'd have to tell me, although I could see he didn't want to.

The cop was walking a few feet behind him, waving his stick and getting more boisterous. "Tell him ah said to git!" the cop bellowed.

Hopper was within a few feet of me now. He took a deep breath and said, "Jackie — ah — the cops says — ".

But before he could say any more, I threw up my hand to save him the embarrassment. "Okay, Skipper," I said, using my best imitation of a Southern drawl, "tell him that ah'm a-gittin'."

And I headed for the shower room with Johnny Wright on my heels.

2

A Black Man in White Baseball

10

WENDELL SMITH

It Was a Great Day in Jersey

Pittsburgh Courier, *April 27, 1946*

The irony of a black man integrating American baseball from a team based outside the United States was not lost on the black press: The supposed cradle of democracy sent the first African American player to Canada before letting him play in America. Even so, April 18, 1946, marked the death of Jim Crow on the ball field in the United States. Robinson turned in a stellar performance at second base with the Montreal Royals in his International League debut in Jersey City against the Giants, the minor league affiliate of the New York Giants. This excerpt from The Sports Beat, Wendell Smith's regular column in the Pittsburgh Courier, highlights Robinson's efforts and Smith's exuberant, ellipsis-sprinkled writing style. The Pittsburgh Courier, published from 1910 to 1966, was the most widely circulated newspaper for African Americans in the United States. Its readership peaked at 450,000 in the 1930s, and it had employees in fourteen cities.

Jersey City, N.J.—The sun smiled down brilliantly in picturesque Roosevelt Stadium here Thursday afternoon and an air of excitement prevailed throughout the spacious park, which was jammed to capacity with 25,000 jabbering, chattering opening day fans . . . A seething mass

From Wendell Smith, "It Was a Great Day in Jersey," The Sports Beat, *Pittsburgh Courier*, April 27, 1946, 26.

of humanity, representing all segments of the crazy-quilt we call America, poured into the magnificent ball park they named after a man from Hyde Park—Franklin D. Roosevelt—to see Montreal play Jersey City and the first two Negroes in modern baseball history perform, Jackie Robinson and Johnny Wright . . . There was the usual fanfare and color, with Mayor Frank Hague chucking out the first ball, the band music, kids from Jersey City schools putting on an exhibition of running, jumping, and acrobatics . . . There was also the hot dogs, peanuts, and soda pop . . . And some guys in the distant bleachers whistled merrily: "Take Me Out to the Ball Game" . . . Wendell Willkie's "One World"[1] was right here on the banks of the Passaic River.

The outfield was dressed in a gaudy green, and the infield was as smooth and clean as a newborn babe . . . And everyone sensed the significance of the occasion as Robinson and Wright marched with the Montreal team to deep centerfield for the raising of the Stars and Stripes and the "Star-Spangled Banner" . . . Mayor Hague strutted proudly with his henchmen flanking him on the right and left . . . While the two teams, spread across the field, marched side by side with military precision, and the band played on . . . We all stood up—25,000 of us—when the band struck up the National Anthem . . . And we sang lustily and freely for this was a great day . . . Robinson and Wright stood out there with the rest of the players and dignitaries, clutching their blue-crowned baseball caps, standing erect and as still as West Point cadets on dress parade.

What Were They Thinking About?

No one will ever know what they were thinking right then, but I have traveled more than 2,000 miles with [these] courageous pioneers during the past nine weeks—from Sanford, Fla. to Daytona Beach to Jersey City—and I feel that I know them probably better than any newspaperman in the business . . . I know that their hearts throbbed heavily and thumped a steady tempo with the big drum that was pounding out the rhythm as the flag slowly crawled up the centerfield mast.

And then there was a tremendous roar as the flag reached its crest and unfurled gloriously in the brilliant April sunlight . . . The 25,000 fans settled back in their seats, ready for the ball game as the Jersey City

---

[1] A liberal Republican onetime presidential candidate, Willkie traveled the globe and wrote *One World* (1943), in which he advocated for an end to colonialism and the establishment of a world government. He also addressed the NAACP, making him one of the most prominent politicians to do so at the time, and was an early white advocate of black civil rights.

Giants jogged out to their positions . . . Robinson was the second batter and as he strolled to the plate the crowd gave him an enthusiastic reception . . . They were for him . . . They all knew how he had overcome many obstacles in the deep South, how he had been barred from playing in Sanford, Fla., Jacksonville, Savannah, and Richmond . . . And yet, through it all, he was standing at the plate as the second baseman of the Montreal team . . . The applause they gave so willingly was a salute of appreciation and admiration . . . Robinson then socked a sizzler to the shortstop and was thrown out by an eye-lash at first base.

The second time he appeared at the plate marked the beginning of what can develop into a great career. He got his first hit as a member of the Montreal Royals . . . It was a mighty home run over the left field fence . . . With two mates on the base paths, he walloped the first pitch that came his way and there was an explosive "crack" as bat and ball met . . . The ball glistened brilliantly in the afternoon sun as it went hurtling high and far over the leftfield fence . . . And, the white flag on the foul-line pole in left fluttered lazily as the ball whistled by.

He Got a Great Ovation from Team, Fans

Robinson jogged around the bases—his heart singing, a broad smile on his beaming bronze face as his two teammates trotted homeward ahead of him . . . When he rounded third, Manager Clay Hopper, who was coaching there, gave him a heavy pat on the back and shouted: "That's the way to hit that ball!" . . . Between third and home-plate, he received another ovation from the stands, and then the entire Montreal team stood up and welcomed him to the bench . . . White hands slapping him on his broad back . . . Deep Southern voices from the bench shouted "Yo sho' hit 'at one, Robbie, nice goin' kid." . . . Another said: "Them folks 'at wouldn't let you play down in Jacksonville should be hee'an now. Whoopee!" . . . And still another: "They cain't stop ya now, Jackie, you're really goin' places, and we're going to be right there with ya!" . . . Jackie Robinson laughed softly and smiled . . . Johnny Wright, wearing a big blue pitcher's jacket, laughed and smiled . . . And, high up in the press box, Joe Bostic of the *Amsterdam News* and I looked at each other knowingly and, we too, laughed and smiled . . . Our hearts beat just a bit faster, and the thrill ran through us like champagne bubbles . . . It was a great day in Jersey . . . It was a great day in baseball! . . .

When the game ended and Montreal had chalked up a 14 to 1 triumph, Robinson dashed for the club house and the showers . . . But before he could get there he was surrounded by a howling mob of kids who came streaming out of the bleachers and stands . . . They swept down upon him like a great ocean wave and he was drowned in a sea of adolescent enthusiasm . . . There he was—this Pied Piper of the diamond—perspiration rolling off his bronze brow, idolizing kids swirling all around him, autograph hounds tugging at him . . . And big cops riding prancing steeds trying unsuccessfully to dispense the mob that had cornered the hero of the day . . . One of his own teammates fought his way through the howling mob and finally "saved" Robinson. . . .

So, Jackie Robinson . . . finally made his way to the dressing room. Bedlam broke loose in there, too . . . Photographers, reporters, kibitzers,[2] and hangers-on fenced him in . . . It was a virtual madhouse. . . . Flash bulbs flashed and reporters fired questions with machine-gun like rapidity . . . And Jackie Robinson smiled through it all.

As he left the park and walked out onto the street, the once-brilliant sun was fading slowly in the distant western skies . . . His petite and dainty little wife greeted him warmly and kindly. "You've had quite a day, little man," she said sweetly.

"Yes," he said softly and pleasantly, "God has been good to us today!"

[2] Yiddish term for people who offer unsolicited advice.

11

CHICAGO DEFENDER

NAACP Youth Group Boycotts Dixie Club

May 25, 1946

Perceiving the long-term ramifications of baseball integration on American society, the NAACP actively supported Robinson's efforts. The protest described in this article from the Chicago Defender *was one of many lodged against racism. The* Chicago Defender, *founded in 1905 and the United States' most influential African American newspaper by the start of World War I in 1914, used vigorous marketing techniques, including*

From "NAACP Youth Group Boycotts Dixie Club," *Chicago Defender*, May 25, 1946, 3.

sensational headlines. At its height, its circulation surpassed 100,000 read-ers, two-thirds of them outside the Chicago area.

Savannah, Ga.—More than 1,000 young people this week attended an NAACP Youth Council meeting and endorsed a resolution to boycott the Savannah Ball Club [the Double-A affiliate of the Cleveland Indians] for discriminating against Jackie Robinson of the Montrealers [by not allowing him to take the field]. . . .

The resolution declared that the action of the Savannah Baseball Club, in conjunction with the city council, was against not only Negro ball players but the entire Negro population: that the club did not deserve the support of Negro fans and that all Savannah Negroes were urged to refrain from attending games at the Municipal Stadium.

12

JOINT MAJOR LEAGUE STEERING COMMITTEE

Report to Commissioner of Baseball A. B. Chandler

August 27, 1946

Even in the summer of 1946, as Robinson played in the white minor leagues as a member of the Montreal Royals, the major league owners expressed their reluctance to accept African American players. In this report delivered to Commissioner of Baseball Albert Benjamin "Happy" Chandler, a committee took up the "race question" as part of a wide-ranging study of key issues affecting major league baseball. The commit-tee was comprised of National League president Ford Frick, American League president William Harridge, and four chief executives, including the New York Yankees' Larry MacPhail. Although the report was issued in segments and never officially as a complete document, it reveals the attitudes of baseball decision makers on race and integration. Ignoring the recommendations of the La Guardia committee from the year before,

From Joint Major League Steering Committee, Report to Commissioner of Baseball A. B. Chandler, August 27, 1946, 18–20.

they had no plans to further the cause against Jim Crow beyond allowing Robinson to play with Montreal at the minor league level.

The appeal of Baseball is not limited to any racial group. The Negro takes great interest in baseball and is, and always has been, among the most loyal supporters of Professional Baseball.[1]

The American people are primarily concerned with the excellence of performance in sport rather than the color, race, or creed of the performer. The history of American sport has been enriched by the performance of great Negro athletes who have attained the mythical All-American team in football; who have won world championships in boxing; and who have helped carry America to track and field victory in the Olympic games. Fifty-four professional Negro baseball players served in the Armed Forces in this war — one player was killed and several wounded in combat.

Baseball will jeopardize its leadership in professional sport if it fails to give full appreciation to the fact that the Negro fan and the Negro player are part and parcel of the game. Certain groups in this country, including political and social-minded drum-beaters, are conducting pressure campaigns in an attempt to force major league clubs to sign Negro players. Members of these groups are not primarily interested in Professional Baseball. They are not campaigning to provide a better opportunity for thousands of Negro boys who want to play baseball. They are not even particularly interested in improving the lot of Negro players who are already employed. They know little about baseball — and nothing about the business and of its operation. They single out Professional Baseball for attack because it offers a good publicity medium.

These people who charge that baseball is flying a Jim Crow flag at its masthead — or that racial discrimination is the basic reason for failure of the major leagues to give employment to Negroes — are simply talking through their individual and collective hats. Professional Baseball is a private business enterprise. It has to depend on profits for its existence, just like any other business. It is a business in which Negroes, as well as Whites, have substantial investments in parks, franchises, and players' contracts. Professional baseball, both Negro and White, has grown and prospered over a period of many years on the basis of separate leagues. The employment of a Negro [Robinson] on one AAA League

---

[1] That is, all-white organized baseball.

Club in 1946 resulted in a tremendous increase in Negro attendance at all games in which the player appeared. The percentage of Negro attendance at some games at Newark and Baltimore was in excess of 50%. A situation might be presented, if Negroes participate in Major League games, in which the preponderance of Negro attendance in parks such as Yankee Stadium, the Polo Grounds, and Comiskey Park could conceivably threaten the value of the Major League franchises owned by these Clubs.

The thousands of Negro boys of ability who aspire to careers in professional baseball should have a better opportunity. Every American boy, without regard to his race or his color or his creed, should have a fair chance in Baseball. Jobs for half a dozen good Negro players now employed in the Negro leagues are relatively unimportant. Signing a few Negro players for the major leagues would be a gesture—but it would contribute little or nothing towards a solution of the real problem. Let's look at the facts:

1. A major league baseball player must have something besides great natural ability. He must possess the technique, the co-ordination, the competitive aptitude, and the discipline, which is usually acquired only after years of training in the minor leagues. The minor league experience of players on the major league rosters, for instance, averages 7 years. The young Negro player never has had a good chance in baseball. Comparatively few good young Negro players are being developed. This is the reason there are not more players who meet major league standards in the big Negro leagues. . . .

2. About 400 Negro professionals are under contract to the 24 clubs in 4 Negro leagues. The Negro leagues have made substantial progress in recent years. Negro baseball is now a $2,000,000 business. One club, the Kansas City Monarchs, drew over 300,000 people to its home and road games in 1944 and 1945. Over 50,000 people paid $72,000 to witness the East–West game at the White Sox Stadium in Chicago. A Negro league game established the all-time attendance record at Griffith Stadium in Washington. The average attendance at Negro games in Yankee Stadium is over 10,000 per game.

These Negro leagues cannot exist without good players. If they cannot field good teams, they will not continue to attract the fans who click the turnstiles. Continued prosperity depends upon improving standards of play. If the major leagues and big minors of Professional Baseball raid these leagues and take their best players—the Negro leagues will eventually fold up—the investments of their club owners will be wiped out—and a lot of professional Negro players will lose their jobs. The

Negroes who own and operate these clubs do not want to part with their outstanding players — no one accuses them of racial discrimination.

3. The Negro leagues rent their parks in many cities from clubs in Organized Baseball. Many major and minor league clubs derive substantial revenue from these rentals. (The Yankee Organization, for instance, nets nearly $100,000 a year from rentals and concessions in connection with Negro league games at Yankee Stadium in New York — and in Newark, Kansas City, and Norfolk). Club owners in the major leagues are reluctant to give up revenues amounting to hundreds of thousands of dollars every year. They naturally want the Negro leagues to continue. They do not sign, and cannot properly sign, players under contract to Negro clubs. This is not racial discrimination. It's simply respecting the contractual relationship between the Negro leagues and their players.

Summary:
Your Committee believes that the relationship of the Negro player and/ or the existing Negro Leagues to professional Baseball is a real problem — one that affects all Baseball — and one that should have serious consideration by an Executive Council.

There are many factors in this problem and many difficulties which will have to be solved before any generally satisfactory solution can be worked out. The individual action of any one Club may exert tremendous pressures upon the whole structure of Professional Baseball, and could conceivably result in lessening the value of several major league franchises.

Your Committee does not desire to question the motives of any organization or individual who is sincerely opposed to segregation or who believes that such a policy is detrimental to the best interests of Professional Baseball.

Your Committee wishes to go on record as feeling that this is an overall problem which vitally affects each and everyone of us — and that effort should be made to arrive at a fair and just solution — compatible with good business judgment and the principles of good sportsmanship.

13

PITTSBURGH COURIER

Big Leaguers Put Okay on Robinson

October 12, 1946

Branch Rickey listed six criteria for the experiment of baseball integration to work. The first two were whether white and black fans alike would accept an African American. Others included the positive reaction of the press, the availability of an open spot on the roster, and the candidate making a good impression off the field. Finally, Rickey believed that the choice came down to pure talent: Could the player compete at the level of whites and thereby earn the respect of his teammates? Robinson had clearly proven his worth to the Montreal Royals, propelling them in 1946 to a 100–54 record, 18½ games ahead of second-place Syracuse, and the International League championship. He was voted the Most Valuable Player in the International League, and owners and players alike noted his talents. He attracted fans to the ballparks — overall, the International League played to a total of more than 2.3 million spectators, an increase of 60 percent over 1945 and 53 percent higher than the previous record, in 1928 — and thus raised revenue for Rickey. At the end of Robinson's first season in organized baseball, Rickey was gratified by reports like this one. Published in the influential black newspaper the Pittsburgh Courier, *it covers one game in the postseason All-Star exhibition circuit that Robinson led. In this game, his minor league squad defeated a team of major leaguers. Of note are the comments of the white players, who assumed that Robinson would be promoted to the majors.*

Jackie Robinson made his Pittsburgh debut in an impressive manner Tuesday afternoon at Forbes Field by leading his All Stars to a 6 to 4 triumph over Honus Wagner's[1] National League All Stars.

[1] Considered one of the greatest shortstops and hitters of all time, Honus Wagner spent nearly his entire career (1897–1917) with the Pittsburgh Pirates. Wagner was one of the original five inductees into the Baseball Hall of Fame.

From "Big Leaguers Put Okay on Robinson," *Pittsburgh Courier*, October 12, 1946, 26.

The Montreal star took a liking to the offerings of Cincinnati's Joe Beggs and connected for three hits. He also stole third base and played a brilliant game at shortstop.

The majority of major leaguers who performed against Robinson agreed that he has what it takes to make the big leagues.

Joe Beggs, brilliant Cincinnati hurler [pitcher], said: "Robinson looks like a real ball player. I'm sure he can make the grade."

Frankie Gustine, Pittsburgh Pirates second baseman, lauded Robinson. "He looks like a big leaguer now," Gustine said. "He can hit and field with the best of them. I think he'll do all right with Brooklyn next year."

Eppie Miller, Cincinnati shortstop, was also impressed with the Negro star. "He should make the grade easily," he declared. "Robinson looks like a great ball player."

MAJORS	ab.	r.	h.	p.	ROBINSON[2]	ab.	r.	h.	p.
Gionfriddo.cf	4	0	0	0	Rackley.cf. . . .	3	1	2	0
*Ortz.lf.	1	1	0	0	Robinson.ss. .	4	3	3	3
Gustine.2b. . .	3	0	1	4	Doby.2b.	3	1	1	5
Lukon.rf-cf. . .	3	0	2	0	Irvin.cf.	3	0	0	2
Bauer.lf.	4	0	0	1	Campanella. c.	4	0	0	4
Suder.ss.	3	0	1	2	Pearson.1b. . .	3	0	2	9
Miller.1b. . . .	4	0	0	10	Souell.3b.	2	0	0	1
Handley.3b. .	4	1	1	3	J.Scott.rf.	4	1	1	3
Susce. c.	4	1	1	4	W.Pope.p	2	1	1	0
Beggs. p.	4	1	0	0	Mindy.p	2	0	0	0
Totals	34	4	6	24	Totals	30	6	10	27

*Ran for Gionfriddo in 5th.

[2] Abbreviations: ab = at bat (The number of times a player came to bat, or made a plate appearance, except for a restricted number of circumstances, including recording a sacrifice hit or walk); r = number of runs scored; h = number of hits; p = putouts, or fielding outs made by the player. The name of each player is followed by his position. For example, Rackley, cf, played center field, and Robinson, ss, played shortstop. The box score shows that Robinson came to bat 4 times, scored 3 runs, had 3 hits, and put out the opposing batter or runner 3 times during the game.

14

CHICAGO DEFENDER

Adventures in Race Relations
November 2, 1946

On the playing field and off it, Jackie Robinson did everything right in the 1946 season, including playing a leading role in his team's championship. The editorial writer of this regular column in the black Chicago Defender, Adventures in Race Relations, *also mentions the continued slights to Robinson.*

Jackie Robinson, first colored athlete in modern times to break into the baseball big leagues, has made good. He led the Montreal team of the International League to its first league championship, and led the league in batting. In the Little World Series[1] where Montreal won its first championship from Louisville of the Southern League, he was superb. Louisville fans booed him and Louisville players deliberately tried to spike him on base slides, but he just grinned and drove in runs. In the fourth and fifth games, he was practically a one-man team. When it was all over, teammates and fans lifted him high on shoulders and paraded him around.

Management of the Brooklyn Dodgers . . . said the only reason he was not brought up to aid the Dodgers in beating off the last ditch challenge of the successful Cardinals was that it would have ruined Montreal's chances for a championship.

And yet—here we go again—when an official league photo was taken of Montreal players, only white players were grouped in the balanced formation. The front row was seated, the back row standing just behind the chairs. Away out on one end, not near any player, the only player not behind the chairs, and throwing the picture out of balance, stood Jackie. The background is plain and our photographer friends say

---

[1] So called because it was the minor league championship; the "big" World Series was for the major leagues.

From "Knuckling," Adventures in Race Relations, *Chicago Defender*, November 2, 1946, 15.

it is child's play to simply blot Jackie off if you want to print the picture without him. And that is exactly what happened when Montreal pictures appeared in Southern papers. Next year, we expect to see Jackie in the middle of the Montreal, or maybe the Dodgers, players.

15

JACKIE ROBINSON

Jackie Robinson Says

Pittsburgh Courier, *April 5, 1947*

Robinson tried to answer the critics and doubters as the 1947 regular season neared and he had not yet been signed to play for the Brooklyn Dodgers. Normally mute on the issue of race in order to meet Rickey's demand to avoid provocation, Robinson explained his frustrations in this piece from Jackie Robinson Says, the regular column in the Pittsburgh Courier *that Wendell Smith likely recruited Robinson to write.*

Every time I pick up a newspaper and read where there may be trouble if or when I am promoted to the big leagues, I have to stop and ask myself why.

As a youngster, I grew up in a territory where I was accepted in athletics for what I could do. It was a democratic sort of thing and I played with youngsters of all races and nationalities without being questioned. If I was good enough, I played. If not, I had to give way to some other kid.

But now, since being accepted in Organized Baseball, most of the articles I read are based mostly on my color. It seems to me that playing baseball is one thing and the color of a man's skin is another. It is discouraging at times to think that I spent thirty-one months in the United

Jackie Robinson, "Jackie Robinson Says," *Pittsburgh Courier*, April 5, 1947, 14.

States Army for the "Four Freedoms"[1] and then when I try to make an honest living playing baseball, I must first be submitted to a "racial test."

Thankful for Good People

Some times I feel like calling it quits. But something urges me on. Perhaps it's because I know there are so many good people pulling for me, both colored and white. Then again, it may be that I can't forget my newly-born son and want to do something for him; something, if possible, to make the way easier for him when he grows up.

I also want to prove to those who resent me or other members of my race that we are not bad people at all. I want to prove that God alone has the right to judge a person and that He is the one who decides people's fates.

I think I can play in the big leagues. All I am asking for is the opportunity. If I fail, I'll step aside and try to do something else.

The training season has ended. I'm now ready for the chance to play with Brooklyn. I hope the color of my skin won't turn out to be my greatest error!

---

[1] President Franklin Roosevelt identified them in 1941 as the freedom of speech and worship and the freedom from want and fear. They became the goals of American foreign policy and the basis of the United Nations' Universal Declaration of Human Rights in 1948.

16

LOUIS EFFRAT

Royals' Star Signs with Brooks Today

New York Times, *April 11, 1947*

The announcement that a black man had signed a contract with a major league club, the first time in the twentieth century that an African American would play at that level, was a topic covered by every news organization. A regular sportswriter for the New York Times, *Louis*

From Louis Effrat, "Royals' Star Signs with Brooks Today," *New York Times*, April 11, 1947, 20.

Effrat reported on the first televised sporting event, a college baseball game between Princeton and Columbia, on May 17, 1939. Covering the three New York baseball teams (as well as all major sports), Effrat was, not surprisingly, called upon to write on the Robinson story.

Jackie Robinson, 28-year-old infielder, yesterday became the first Negro to achieve major-league status in modern times. His contract was purchased from the Montreal Royals of the International League by the Dodgers and he will be in a Brooklyn uniform at Ebbets Field today, when the Brooks [Brooklyn Dodgers] oppose the Yankees in the first of three exhibition games over the week-end. . . .

The decision was made while Robinson was playing first base for Montreal against the Dodgers at Ebbets Field. Jackie was blanked at the plate and contributed little to his team's 4–3 victory before 14,282 fans, but it was nevertheless a history-making day for the well-proportioned lad.

An Inopportune Moment

Jackie had just popped into a double-play,[1] attempting to bunt in the fifth inning, when Arthur Mann, assistant to Rickey, appeared in the press box. He handed out a brief, typed announcement: "The Brooklyn Dodgers today purchased the contract of Jackie Roosevelt Robinson from the Montreal Royals."

Robinson will appear at the Brooklyn offices this morning to sign a contract. Rickey does not anticipate any difficulty over terms.

According to the records, the last Negro to play in the majors was one Moses Fleetwood Walker, who caught [played catcher] for Toledo of the American Association when that circuit enjoyed major-league classification back in 1884.

The call for Robinson was no surprise. Most baseball persons had been expecting it. After all, he had proved his right to the opportunity by his extraordinary work in the AAA minor league, where he stole 40 bases and was the best defensive second baseman. He sparked the Royals to the pennant [league championship] and the team went on to annex the little world series.

Robinson's path in the immediate future may not be too smooth, however. He may run into antipathy from Southerners, who form about

---

[1] A bad result for a hitter, in which he causes two outs from one at bat.

60 per cent of the league's playing strength. In fact, it is rumored that a number of Dodgers expressed themselves unhappy at the possibility of having to play with Jackie.

Robinson Is "Thrilled"

Jackie, himself, expects no trouble. He said he was "thrilled and it's what I've been waiting for." When his Montreal mates congratulated him and wished him luck, Robinson answered, "Thanks, I'll need it."

Whether Robinson will be used at first or second base is not known. That will depend upon the new manager, yet to be named by Rickey.

Rickey, in answer to a direct query, declared he did not expect trouble from other players because of Robinson. "We are all agreed," he said, "that Jackie is ready for the chance."

Several thousand Negroes were in the stands at yesterday's exhibition. When Robinson appeared for batting practice, he drew a warm and pleasant reception. Dixie Walker, quoted in 1945 as opposed to playing with Jackie, was booed on his first turn at bat. Walker answered with a resounding single.

If, however, Robinson is to make the grade, he will have to do better than he did against the Brooks. Against [pitcher] Ralph Branca, Jackie rolled meekly to the mound, walked, and then popped an intended sacrifice bunt into a double play. At first base—a new position for him—he handled himself flawlessly, but did not have a difficult chance.[2]

---

[2] That is, he did not face any challenging plays.

17

JACKIE ROBINSON

Jackie Robinson Says

Pittsburgh Courier, *April 19, 1947*

On April 15, 1947, Jackie Robinson became the first black man since Moses Fleetwood Walker in 1888 to appear in an official major league game. African American newspapers covered the event from every angle. In this piece from his column in the Pittsburgh Courier *(see Document 15), and likely aided by the eloquent Wendell Smith, Robinson relates the whirlwind of events from his signing to his debut with the Brooklyn Dodgers five days later.*

Brooklyn, N.Y.—Next time I go to a movie and see a picture of a little ordinary girl become a great star, I'll believe it.

And whenever I hear my wife read fairy tales to my little boy, I'll listen.

I know now that dreams do come true.

I know because I am now playing with the Brooklyn Dodgers in the big leagues!

I always dreamed about playing for the Dodgers but, honestly, I always had my doubts. I used to tell myself: "Something will happen. It just isn't in the books for you to play in the majors. You're a Negro. Negroes haven't been in the big leagues. Some day they will be. But you won't be the lucky guy."

Then last Thursday, Mr. Rickey called me to his office. He said: "Jackie, you're a big leaguer now. You're going to play with the Dodgers and we're announcing it to the world today."

In a Trance

I walked out of his office in a trance. I went from there to Ebbets Field to play my last game with Montreal against Brooklyn. I don't think I was too impressive in that last game with Montreal. But that was because, I guess, I couldn't keep my mind on the game all the time. Every time I'd

---

Jackie Robinson, "Jackie Robinson Says," *Pittsburgh Courier*, April 19, 1947, 18.

look at Pee Wee Reese or Bruce Edwards, or Ed Head[1] and the other Dodgers, I'd start thinking.

"Just think," I'd say to myself, "tomorrow I'll be with them. I'll be wearing a Brooklyn uniform." And then I'd look at the big park and realize that I would be here this year—playing in a major league park before big crowds and fighting for a pennant.

At noon Friday, I walked into the Brooklyn clubhouse. When I opened that door, I walked into the major leagues, and a few minutes later I was dressing with big league players and getting ready to play against the famous Yankees.

Then we went out on the field. Gee it seemed big. Twice as big as the day before. I sat down in the Brooklyn dugout and started to think all over again. The game started and I found myself at first base. I was the Brooklyn first baseman. The day before, I had been Montreal's first baseman. "What a difference a day makes," I said to myself.

When the umpire said: "Play ball!," I finally started thinking baseball. I finally realized that I was a member of the Brooklyn Dodgers; that I had made the big leagues.

Realized Responsibility

When I realized that, the thrill was gone. I knew that from then on, I'll have to play like the very devil. So now I'm trying my best. I don't know how successful I'll be, but you can bet that I'll give my level best. I think I can do a good enough job to stay up here and face such teams as the Cardinals, Pirates, Giants, and the rest. I'm new and have a lot to learn, but I've found out that there are fellows on the club willing to help me. Ed Stanky,[2] a great ball player, helped me the first day. Others have advised me and coached me since. I know by that experience that I'm not alone. I also know by the applause I've received in these first games that the public is for me and wants to see me make good.

I will never stop trying. I hope I'll get better and better every day and help bring a pennant and a world series to Brooklyn.

Being up here is absolutely wonderful. That's why I'm a believer in fairy tales now. You see, it actually happened to me.

—HE MADE IT!—

---

[1] Reese was the shortstop, and Edwards was the catcher. Pitcher Ed Head gave up no hits in his first game in 1946 but failed to make the team after spring training in 1947 and never pitched in the majors again.

[2] A southerner, the feisty Stanky eventually defended Robinson from racial slurs. He started at second base, which forced Robinson to play first base in 1947. When Stanky was traded to the Boston Braves the next season, Robinson moved to second.

3

Responses to the Great Experiment

18

NEW YORK AMSTERDAM NEWS

Let's Help Jackie Do It!

April 19, 1947

As this editorial from the major New York City black newspaper reveals, the black press took to heart Rickey's admonition that African Americans behave with moderation toward Robinson's appearance so as not to provoke the rage, disdain, or anxiety of whites.

All of Brooklyn, as well as thousands throughout the country, are rooting heart and soul for Jackie Robinson, first Negro in Major Leagues, to come through with colors flying. Naturally, we are optimistic and feel that Jackie's natural ability and all-around knowledge of the game will terminate in an abundance of success.

While Jackie will be playing his heart out on the field, opening the door for other talented Negro baseball players, it will be up to us to do our part in the stands. We must be an asset to him and make him feel proud of us at all times.

This editorial is not directed to the thousands who are well aware of the conduct that is required at the various ballparks, but is chiefly pointed to those unthoughtful fans who think the stands are three-ring circuses and that they are part of the circus. Those ridiculous loud and uncouth jokes and those fanatic dances must go.

"Let's Help Jackie Do It!!!," editorial, *New York Amsterdam News*, April 19, 1947, 14.

Two individuals in the stands on Sunday afternoon made all of us [ashamed]. It would be easier to jot down the things they didn't do than it would be for us to write the things they did.

Jackie will be watched daily with keen eyes as he performs in various parks, and it will be up to us to do our part. We must not let him down. We are proud of him and also proud of ourselves.

There is no need to take the bottle to the stands. Let's take our sip after it is all over—this is the way it should be done. Profanity is not necessary and the grandstands certainly are not picnic grounds.

Don't think that we want you to go to the park and sit like a mummy or portray a saint. We want you to have fun—all the fun there is—but in a clean, healthy manner. We must remember that thousands of our kids who have made Jackie their idol, will be there, too. If we don't act right, they may misinterpret the correct way a fan should act.

As we stated at the start of this editorial, it is not intended for the major portion of fans who are justly proud of Jackie and who know how to conduct themselves at public gatherings, but to the ones who apparently are too "smart" for their own good.

Let us hope, in conclusion, that nothing will happen in the grandstands that will hamper Jackie's progress. We believe and have urged interracial understanding and we will do everything in our power to push forward this conception of American living.

It will be well to remember that we are on the spot just as Jackie. We cannot afford to let him down!!!

19

SPORTING NEWS

A Negro in the Major Leagues

April 23, 1947

The ambivalence of the white baseball press toward Robinson is apparent in this editorial from the Sporting News, *the so-called "bible of baseball," established in 1886 and based in segregated Saint Louis. The writer admires Robinson and baseball's ability to adjust to new societal pressures for equal rights. Yet the editorial also offers a veiled warning that black*

"A Negro in the Major Leagues," editorial, *Sporting News*, April 23, 1947, 12.

*players should make teams only if they possess the necessary talent, not
because of their race. The condescension toward African Americans—the
call to be patient—foreshadows 1960s tensions between moderates, who
sought equality through gradual change, and more militant voices, who
demanded an immediate end to Jim Crow and rapid strides in fair treatment for minorities.*

In the seventy-second year of the National League's history, a Negro has
made his appearance on its player rolls for the first time. Jackie Robinson, brought up from the Montreal farm, is listed as a first baseman with
the Brooklyn club.

Once Robinson had taken the field with the Dodgers, it was remarked
that it was quite odd that a Negro had not been seen in the majors before
in the modern history of the game.

To a sport-loving public which had seen Negroes in professional
football, Negroes in college gridiron competition, and Negroes winning
world boxing championships, Robinson's appearance on a major-league
field hardly was a novelty.

To some of the ballplayers, the entry of a Negro into a field of en-
deavor hitherto closed to that race, albeit open to other non-Caucasians,
admittedly was irksome. But that phase of the situation, too, will pass
and before long we may expect to see any Negro ballplayer worthy of a
place in the major leagues performing in that company.

As Robinson himself admitted when he was purchased by the Brooklyn club, his promotion to the majors involves certain peculiar responsi-
bilities, both for Jackie as an individual, for the Negroes as a race new to
the Big Time, and for exclusively Negro baseball as a possible feeder of
the National and American leagues.

Negro baseball of the past was not too careful about its general conduct. It had no great respect for contracts, for schedules, for a sense of
responsibility to Organized Baseball.

Last year, a Negro report on Negro baseball admitted that Negro players had been guilty of certain irregularities which would not be coun-
tenanced for one minute by the commissioner of Organized Baseball.

It is up to Negro baseball to recognize the elevation of Robinson to
the majors by cleaning house and establishing itself as a clean, well-
conducted feeder of the higher company.

To Robinson, no warning is necessary. He is a well-behaved, highly
understanding man who recognizes his unique position and the fact that
on him rests the burden of persuading Organized Baseball to engage
more players of his race.

To the Negro fan, let it be said that he must approach the new situation with understanding and patience, two qualities his race long has utilized in its amalgamation into American life, especially in the South.

Pitchers undoubtedly will "test" Robinson's gameness, and there will be other incidents which may make the Negro fan angry.

But Robinson will establish his own position and that of his race in baseball as he established it in the Junior World Series last fall against Louisville.

In games in the Kentucky metropolis, Louisville pitchers sorely tried Jackie's temper. But after every trip into the dirt, he came up smiling. He could take it. And eventually, the Colonels forgot Robinson's color and treated him as just another Montreal player.

Jackie Robinson's presence among the Brooklyn personnel marks a vast forward stride for Organized Baseball in the social revolution which has gained a tremendous impetus through the world war.

20

LESTER RODNEY

Interview with Effa Manley

Daily Worker, *April 29, 1947*

In this interview by Lester Rodney, sports editor of the U.S. Communist party's Daily Worker *(see Document 1), Newark Eagles owner Effa Manley expresses her thoughts on integrated baseball and its effects on her Negro League business. As the sole owner of the Eagles (her husband, Abe, had died in 1946) and longtime treasurer of the Negro National League, she was well qualified to speak on such matters. A crusader for civil rights, Manley had led the "Don't Buy Where You Can't Work" boycotts of 1934–1935 that resulted in the hiring of black salesclerks in some three hundred stores in Harlem. She was the only female owner in the Negro Leagues and the first woman inducted (in 2006) into the Baseball Hall of Fame. She would sell the Eagles — characterized as the Dodgers of black baseball for their high profile in the community of Newark — in*

From Lester Rodney, On the Scoreboard, *Daily Worker*, April 29, 1947, 10.

1948, when the "Robinson effect" had begun to devastate the Negro Leagues. The team moved to Houston and lasted until 1950 in the Negro American League.

A native New Yorker who developed a lifelong love for the Brooklyn Dodgers, Lester Rodney had worked at odd jobs after dropping out of Syracuse University to help support his parents, who had lost their jobs during the Great Depression. His only qualification for sportswriting seemingly came from his experience on a high school newspaper. Nevertheless, in 1936 the Daily Worker *hired him as its sports editor, a position from which he launched his crusade to integrate major league baseball. Over his twenty-two-year career at the newspaper, Rodney consistently swiped at the racism and antilabor stance of organized baseball.* On the Scoreboard *was his regular column.*

How about the Negro National League? What effect has the first breaking of big league Jim Crow had on it, if any? Is it true, as some say, that the Negro owners are against the big leagues taking ball players from them? I found Mrs. Effa Manley, owner of the championship Newark Eagles, sitting behind home plate well back in the lower grandstands of the Polo Grounds.[1] Her team was playing the New York Cubans of the same league in a pre-season exhibition. . . .

The two Negro leagues were born fourteen years ago out of Jim Crow and a supply of talented, frustrated athletes. Many players good enough to play in the big leagues have come and gone, some jump to Mexico, Cuba, and Venezuela for more money than the Negro magnates can pay and the greatest of them all was a man named Satchel Paige, who was born too soon to be known as the best big league pitcher of all time but who will surely be remembered as the best by all who saw him in his prime.[2]

The teams in the Negro leagues generally hire major and minor league ball parks at a goodly rental when the home clubs are away and though they play in comparative obscurity, with hardly any mention in the regular press, they draw surprisingly large crowds, about 85 percent Negro. Disconnected from the methodical training, conditioning, and experiences of the big leagues, the caliber of play is uneven but exciting and on the whole, approximate that of a good Class A minor league.

---

[1] The New York Giants' ballpark.
[2] Satchel Paige did make the big leagues, signing with the Cleveland Indians in 1948.

Mrs. Manley, a handsome woman in her forties who [has owned] the Eagles for eleven years, was glad to talk about things to a reporter, though she's so intent a fan it became judicious to ask questions only between innings when the teams were changing positions.

Knows Her Baseball

Before talking about Robinson, the Dodgers, and the feelings of the Negro club owners, it was natural enough to chat about the teams and the game down on the field in front of us. . . .

She spoke with enthusiasm ("he has everything!") of Monte Irvin,[3] Newark centerfielder who led the league in '45 with a rousing .389 [batting average] and who poled out two singles and a home run this day. She also liked Larry Doby,[4] second baseman who would look sweet on several big league clubs, I could (and will) mention. . . .

"We're going to play at Ebbets Field this year," Mrs. Manley said. "Our first series there is May 30 and I hope some white fans come out to see us."

Which led to the big question . . . and its answer.

"I can certainly speak for myself," she said with a decided emphasis. "I'm all for it. Branch Rickey is to be congratulated. I wouldn't be selfish enough to stand in the way of any player who could better himself. Why three of my best, Day,[5] Ruffin,[6] and Dandridge,[7] went to Mexico this season to take good offers and I was happy for them.

---

[3] This Hall of Fame outfielder played for Newark from 1938 to 1942 and again (after service in the war) from 1945 to 1948 before joining the New York Giants in 1949. A perennial Negro League All-Star, Irvin played on the team that won the Negro World Series in 1946 and was with the Giants when they won the World Series in 1954. When Rickey approached Manley about signing Irvin, she refused, noting that Rickey had hired Robinson without any compensation to Negro League owners. Eventually, the Giants likewise signed Irvin, without paying Manley for the rights to his contract.

[4] Doby played for the Newark Eagles in 1942–1943 and 1946–1947. The first black player in the American League, Doby signed with the Cleveland Indians in July 1947 and remained with them until 1955, when he left for the Chicago White Sox for two seasons. Doby returned to the Indians for 1958, then played with the Detroit Tigers and White Sox before retiring from the majors. He was elected to the Hall of Fame in 1998.

[5] Hall of Famer Leon Day was a premier Negro National League pitcher who played for teams in Baltimore, Newark, and Philadelphia from 1935 to 1950 (interrupted by war service). Day had stints in Mexico and Canada as well and reached the U.S. minor leagues in 1951–1952. He compiled a perfect 13–0 record for the Newark Eagles in 1937.

[6] Catcher Charles Ruffin played in the Negro Leagues from 1935 to 1946, mostly with Newark.

[7] Ray Dandridge was elected to the Hall of Fame as one of the great infielders in history. Too old to play in the majors, this black star had played for Newark in the 1930s, but because he felt the Manleys underpaid him, he moved to Mexico, where he played

"I don't think we'd have to worry about players if other teams followed Brooklyn's example," she went on. "Opening more opportunities makes more players. Did you know all the Negro colleges are having baseball teams for the first time?

"I personally feel we have built up a following who prefer our league and game, regardless, but it would be a wonderful thing to see full equality of opportunity in the big leagues. All we would want would be a fair price for the players—just as the minor leagues get. Players represent considerable investments."

And there was the answer to the question that brought me to the Polo Grounds. As to how the players themselves feel about the chance to move up and make big league dough, just ask them. I did.

---

for most of the next decade. Dandridge returned to the Eagles for one year (1944), managed the Cubans, and then was a premier player in Triple-A baseball from 1949 to 1955, when he retired.

21

JIMMY CANNON

Lynch Mobs Don't Always Wear Hoods

New York Times, May 13, 1947

The New York–based white sportswriter Jimmy Cannon was known for his coverage of boxing and the unique style in which he wrote on far-ranging issues related to sports (much like his friend and admirer Ernest Hemingway), so much so that he became famous for frequently opening his columns with "Nobody asked me, but . . ." He is invariably ranked as one of the great American sportswriters, noted for the breezy combination of street-tough and sentimental prose—a brawler with a heart of gold—with which he sharply drew character sketches and critical

---

Jimmy Cannon, "Lynch Mobs Don't Always Wear Hoods," *New York Times*, May 13, 1947, 19.

situations. Early to recognize the importance of integration and a harsh critic of Jim Crow, the liberal Cannon memorably called Joe Louis, the black heavyweight boxing champion of the 1930s, "a credit to his race, the human race." Referred to as "America's ace sports editor" in his byline, he was a tireless supporter of erasing the color line in baseball, as is evident in this column from the United States' biggest national newspaper, the New York Times.

You don't always lynch a man by hanging him from a tree. There is a great lynch mob among us and they go unhooded and work without a rope. They have no leader but their own hatred of humanity. They are the quietly degraded, who plot against the helpless with skill and a coward's stealth and without fear of reprisal. Their weapon is as painful as the lash, the hot tar, the noose, or the shotgun. They string up a man with the whisper of a lie and they persecute him with ridicule. They require no burning cross as a signal of assembly and need no sheet to identify themselves to each other. They are the night riders who operate 24 hours a day.

They lynch a man with a calculated contempt which no court of law can consider a crime. Such a venomous conspiracy is the one now trying to run Jackie Robinson out of organized baseball. It does not go for all ball players and not even all the St. Louis Cards, some of whom are accused of trying to arrange a strike to protest against the presence of a Negro in the big league. But such a state exists and we should all be ashamed of it, not only those connected with the sport, but any one who considers this his country. It is an indication, I believe, that as a people, we are a failure and not as good as the laws by which we live.

We are a people guaranteed more freedoms than any other on earth. Yet there are among us some who refute those documents which pledge us the things that people fight for everywhere and rarely achieve. When such persecutions become the aim of a government it is the record of history that men rise in revolt against the leaders of their state. It was to defeat such persecutions that men fought in the undergrounds of Europe and in every righteous army since man first realized freedom is seldom achieved without struggle. We are a people who consider such privileges as ordinary because they were written down in the book for us to live by long ago. But among us are those who consider these liberties as their own and would take them from the defenseless whom they can afford to torment. They form a lynch mob that is out to avenge a right.

Only the stupidly bold among them collect on mountainsides by the light of torches. You find them wherever you go and their lodge is national although they pay no dues and carry no card. It is only natural that baseball, being our country's sport, should be played by some of them because they are in all trades and professions and they carry an invisible rope with them at all times. It is my belief that such a philosophy of hate does not dominate baseball. It if does, then they should burn up all the bats and balls and turn cattle to graze on the outfield grass. Baseball is not a way of life but an escape from it. It is to the bleachers and the grandstands that the multitudes flee to forget the world beyond the fences. Such a haven should not be corrupted by senseless hate, but once it is, baseball has no reason to exist.

Baseball is supported by the people and I have heard them demand justice for Robinson. If their applause is any indication, they ask that Robinson be accepted as an athlete and is entitled to the right to be judged by the scorer's ledger and not by the prejudices of indecent men. It is my belief that Robinson is a big leaguer of ordinary ability. If he is not, then he should be sent down to the minors because it is the opinion of all of us who consider baseball a sport that skill and honesty are the only qualifications a man should have. It is doubtful if Robinson has yet shown his true worth. He came up as a shortstop, was transformed into a second baseman at Montreal, and is now playing first. It is a tribute to his solidness as a man that he hasn't fallen apart as a ball player. Less heart has burned better ball players out of the big leagues. About him rages the silent uproar of a perpetual commotion. He is the most discussed ball player of this time and his judges do not evaluate him for his actions on the field alone. But he has concealed the turmoil within him and when you talk to him there is no indication he regards himself as a special man who faces problems no other big leaguer ever faced before. The times I have spoken to him he has praised all those with whom he plays.

What goes on in the privacy of the hotel rooms where the Dodgers gather I don't know. I have listened to [second baseman] Eddie Stanky praise Robinson for his alertness. Jackie told me himself that [pitcher] Hughie Casey had helped him when he needed practice and advice on making the difficult plays a first baseman must face.

But in the clubhouse Robinson is a stranger. The Dodgers are polite and courteous with him but it is obvious he is isolated by those with whom he plays. I have never heard remarks made against him or detected any rudeness where he was concerned. But the silence is loud and Robinson never is part of the jovial and aimless banter of the locker room. He is the loneliest man I have ever seen in sports.

We have been involved in a war to guarantee all people the right to a life without fear. The peoples of the earth are still assailed by the same doubts and terrors. The old men once more talk of violence and only the dead are sure of peace. In such a world it seems a small thing that a man be able to play a game unmolested. In our time such a plea should be unnecessary. But when it happens we must again remember that all this country's enemies are not beyond the frontiers of our home land.

22

ATLANTA DAILY WORLD

Jackie Robinson Continues to "Pack 'Em In" at Gate

May 27, 1947

Contemporary accounts in the black press, such as this one from the Atlanta Daily World, *substantiate the view that Robinson's presence on the field expanded attendance in the stands. Journalist Wendell Smith (see Document 5) once quipped, "Jackie's nimble, Jackie's quick, Jackie's making the turnstiles click." In the immediate term, Robinson was a boon to attendance in National League parks, but the reality was more complicated. At home, attendance at Dodgers games increased in 1947, but by a mere eleven thousand fans, and it actually declined as a percentage of total National League attendance. In many parks, the largest single-game crowds were actually smaller in 1947 than in 1946. More black fans came out for games, but statistics show that in many cities, the very fact that African Americans showed up was a novelty that led to exaggerated claims of an influx of spectators.*

Founded in 1928, the Atlanta Daily World *had by 1933 expanded from the only black newspaper in the city to the first black daily in the country. Although it covered lynchings, police brutality, and school segregation, the newspaper did not support more aggressive forms of civil*

From "Jackie Robinson Continues to 'Pack 'Em In' at Gate," *Atlanta Daily World*, May 27, 1947, 5.

rights, such as the sit-ins of the 1960s. Thus white businesses felt comfortable advertising in its pages, though activists criticized its timidity.

St. Louis—While the Brooklyn Dodgers have been no ball of fire in winning games on the first western road trip of the current season, their first baseman, Jackie Robinson, has certainly made the turnstiles click.

In the first game of the [Chicago] Cub series there was a paid attendance of 46,572, the largest crowd at Wrigley Field since the days when ropes were stretched around the outfield and fans were allowed on the playing field.

Other high attendance figures include 40,952 paid admissions in Philadelphia and 34,813 cash customers in Pittsburgh on a gloomy threatening night. In April at the Polo Grounds one game against the Giants was played before 52,335 fans.

Increased attendance of colored fans at all games of the Dodgers is noticeable, and if the spirit of Americanism will not move major league magnates to follow the example of Branch Rickey, president, of the Dodgers, and bring capable colored ball players into the big show, the click of the turnstiles, which is music to their ears, might do it.

The presence of Robinson alone in the big leagues is in itself not sufficient. If the color bar is to be outmoded, other colored players will have to be brought into organized baseball so that they can be as freely sold and exchanged in the baseball market as white ball players.

23

Sample of Hate Mail Received
May 20, 1951

Robinson received death threats such as this one, as well as other hate mail. This letter typifies the ongoing intimidation that he and his family faced. It was sent to the president and general manager of the Cincinnati Reds, Warren Giles, who shared its contents with Robinson. On the same day that Giles received and Robinson learned of the letter, the Dodgers swept a doubleheader against the Reds at Cincinnati's Crosley Field; in the first game, Robinson hit a home run. The threat proved harmless, but the FBI investigated the letter nonetheless.

From Jackie Robinson, *First Class Citizenship: The Civil Rights Letters of Jackie Robinson,* ed. Michael G. Long (New York: Times Books, 2007), 10.

24

JACKIE ROBINSON

Jackie Robinson Says

Pittsburgh Courier, *May 17, 1947*

The black press exulted over Robinson and monitored his every step. In his column in the Pittsburgh Courier *(see Document 15), Robinson, under the likely supervision of Wendell Smith, reported to an avid audience on his thoughts and actions during the 1947 season. Regarding negative experiences, what the black press saw as inexcusable racist behavior Robinson explained as no more than a nuisance. His description of the hand-shaking incident with Ben Chapman, manager of the Philadelphia Phillies, disguises Robinson's disgust with Chapman's racial taunts. Police believed that the threats of violence to which Robinson refers were genuine.*

I've been a pretty busy fellow the past week. Between trying to play big league baseball and answering all kinds of questions about alleged strikes and threatening letters, I haven't had much time to do anything else. However, as things are going now, I guess I haven't anything to worry about. By that I mean that everyone I have come in contact with since I joined the Dodgers has been all right. There was a lot of talk once, for instance, about how the Phillies were riding me. In fact, it became an issue. But the other day, a photographer came into our dugout and asked me to go over and have my picture taken with Ben Chapman, manager of the Phillies.

I was glad to cooperate and when we got over to the Phillies' dugout, Chapman came out and shook my hand. We said hello to teach other and he smiled when the picture was snapped. Chapman impressed me as a nice fellow and I don't think he really meant the things he was shouting at me the first time we played Philadelphia.

Jackie Robinson, "Jackie Robinson Says," *Pittsburgh Courier*, May 17, 1947, 14.

I feel much better this week because I've been hitting the ball much better. For a while there, I was hitting in tough luck. But the past week some of my blows have fallen safely and that's the important thing. It is hard enough to get a hit in the big leagues when you're lucky, but when you're not lucky, then it's really tough. When I didn't get a hit for a few games, a lot of my friends started worrying. They kept asking me what was wrong. Well, I couldn't tell them because I didn't know. I was hitting the ball good most of the time, but right into someone's hands. You must remember, too, that big league fielders know how to play hitters. That's why the managers try to teach their hitters to hit the ball to all fields. If you can only hit to left field, for instance, you're going to have a hard time getting safe hits through the infield or outfield. But if you can punch hits to all fields, you're going to have an easier time.

The police wanted to know about some threatening letters I have received. I admit that I've received some, but by the way they were written, I would say they're from scatter-brained people who just want something to yelp about. I am glad to say that for the few nasty letters I've received, I've gotten from ten to twenty more congratulating me and offering me encouragement. Those letters have helped a lot and I'm not worrying about a few "small" people who can't make up their minds whether or not they like living in a Democracy.

25

HENRY FONER

The Meaning of Jackie for the Jewish Race
1998

The Jewish community greatly respected and closely watched the Robinson experiment. In 1947, Henry Foner was the welfare and educational director of the Fur, Leather, and Machine Workers Union; editor of the union's newspaper; and a social activist who also wrote for the journal Jewish Currents. *A former teacher in New York City public high schools, Foner*

From Henry Foner, "Mah Nishtanah," in *Jackie Robinson: Race, Sports, and the American Dream*, ed. Joseph Dorinson and Joram Warmund (Armonk, N.Y.: M. E. Sharpe, 1998), 70–71.

refers in this personal account to the "Rapp-Coudert witchhunt," named after the chairmen of a committee of the New York State legislature that dismissed some forty teachers at City College of New York for supposedly peddling communism in the public education system between 1940 and 1942. Foner was denied a license to teach due to the Rapp-Coudert investigation in 1948 and then went to work for the union. Forty years after witnessing Robinson break the color barrier in Brooklyn, Foner told this story during an event at the New York Public Library. Listening to him in the audience was an assistant to filmmaker Ken Burns, who enlisted Foner to retell the story in Burns's 1994 documentary Baseball. *Later, it was printed as an essay in a book commemorating Robinson's Dodgers debut.*

The year 1947 has already gone down in baseball history as the year in which Jim Crow was sent packing by professional baseball. It will be so designated here in Brooklyn this coming April when the borough marks the fiftieth anniversary of Jackie Robinson's ascension in the major leagues.

For me, it will help keep alive the memory of a day forever etched in my mind. I was a substitute teacher in stenography and typewriting at Prospect Heights High School, six blocks from Ebbets Field. I had a spiritual if not racial kinship with Robinson. Just as he was battling seemingly insurmountable odds to become a big-league baseball player, I was engaged in an uphill struggle to become a "regular" teacher, despite a Rapp-Coudert witchhunt that had already (temporarily) laid waste the careers of my brothers . . . two history professors and one clerk in the registrar's office at City College. . . .

Against this background, it is not surprising that the news of Robinson's exploits struck a particularly responsive chord in me. I couldn't help feeling that fate had placed me within walking distance of a historical event, and, as I drilled my students that day in the fine points of the "l" and "r" hooks in Pitman stenography, I looked forward to my visit to Ebbets Field that afternoon.

Finally, I was seated in the left-field stands. Robinson came out on the field, resplendent in his Montreal uniform. The Royals, then a Dodger farm team, were on hand for an exhibition game and were expected to give up their prize shortstop to their seigniorial lieges at the end of the day. All went according to plan. From my seat in the stands, I watched the brief ceremony on the field marking the tumbling down of the walls of Jim Crow in America's national pastime—and then went home to prepare for my family's Passover seder that evening.

The Foner family seders, being inhabited by scholars and political activists, often became battlegrounds for the expression and rebuttal of various pet theses. On that night, however, things were different. As the youngest in the family, it devolved upon me to ask the *fir kashes*, or four questions. That night, they took on a different meaning. After the first question, "Why is this night different from all other nights?" I . . . replied, "Today, the first black American baseball player entered the major leagues."

26

JAMES A. MANNIX

An Open Letter to Jackie Robinson

New York Amsterdam News, *September 13, 1947*

Although the black press in particular drew lessons from the Robinson experiment, this letter to the editor of the New York Amsterdam News *(see Document 8) expresses the views of a white man, James A. Mannix. We can only surmise that Mannix lived in Brooklyn, as he appears in the historical record only through this letter and an earlier one from about 1940–1945 in the* Brooklyn Eagle *that lauded Brooklyn's Italian community. This letter makes clear, however, Mannix's support of civil rights and the inspiration he drew from Robinson's debut season.*

Dear Jackie:
After you have wiped the perspiration from your courageous brow and have set your bat down for the day, I am hoping you can find time to peruse this letter which is written by a guy who is rounding out his 48th year in the vale of tears in which we have tolerance and intolerance, brother against brother, and yet, some brotherhood.

James A. Mannix, "An Open Letter to Jackie Robinson," editorial, *New York Amsterdam News*, September 13, 1947, 16.

Still, Jackie, there are men like yourself—colored friends of mine and there are Jews and Gentiles who do much during the course of their lives to bring out the sporting blood in men of all races and creeds.

While on vacation, the writer started out last Tuesday for a stroll. A low sultry haze hung over the city like an early morning dew. Standing along the mahogany stick were several men quaffing their cold beer. As I observed these men, all total strangers to me, I knew that they were cold sober. One guy started praising you and cited the great fight and progress you have made in baseball. All the other guys agreed 100%.

Jackie, I have seen so much of a lack of tolerance in my days. I was inclined to wonder if all these fellows felt the same way about you on the first day you went out onto the field with a bat in your hands. So many guys still don't know that the Civil War is over.

But Jackie, do you fully realize what you've done since you put on that uniform? In the very face of narrowness, unfairness, and stupidity, you have gone out on baseball diamonds, taken your bat in your hands, and made good. The balls you batted out went far and high and some people who had narrow minds craned their necks for once and saw the light. You reached their sporting hearts and now they're rooting for you.

Many people of the Colored race faced the same obstacles as yourself, but they came through as doctors, lawyers, judges, scientists and they have been and still are, successes in many other fields as well.

So, keep in there batting, son. And Jackie, just one more thought. Another fellow who has brought great credit to your race made a remark during the last war—a remark never to be forgotten. Said he, "God is on our side."

No finer, cleaner American who has done so much to increase confidence and respect within sporting circles can beat Joe Louis.[1] Joe and Babe Ruth[2] will be remembered and respected long after a lot of us have walked into the silent valley.

I'd like to borrow Joe's words and say to you, remember that each day and night that you take your bat into your hands—God is on your side. So, stay in there batting and keep up the swell job you are doing. Don't let Him down and don't let any of us down!

---

[1] Black heavyweight boxing champion in the 1930s who backed Robinson's integration efforts.

[2] A record-holding home run hitter and cultural icon, George Herman "Babe" Ruth was one of the first group of players inducted in 1936 into the Baseball Hall of Fame. Diagnosed with cancer the year before this letter appeared, Ruth died in August 1948.

27

ROY WILKINS

The Watchtower

Los Angeles Sentinel, *January 1, 1948*

A newcomer relative to other big-city black newspapers, the Los Angeles Sentinel *was established in 1933 but had reached a sizable circulation by 1947. After working as editor of the* Call *in Kansas City, Roy Wilkins joined the NAACP and replaced W. E. B. Du Bois as editor of its magazine, the* Crisis, *in 1934. In 1950, he chaired the National Emergency Civil Rights Conference, a meeting attended by more than one hundred activist groups, and the next year he helped found the Leadership Conference on Civil Rights, which led the campaigns for civil rights bills thereafter. Wilkins's rise in the NAACP culminated in his appointment as executive director in 1964. This article comes from The Watchtower, a regular editorial column by Wilkins that ran in several black newspapers during the 1940s.*

The year just past was marked by smashing attacks on the ideas that have held Negroes in second class American citizenship. Moreover, 1947 saw almost unbelievable progress in cracking the patterns that have shackled the dark brother.

History will show that it was in 1947 that the old idea of equality under segregation took its first powerful, public socks on the chin. Hitherto, although there were always voices crying in the wilderness, spearheaded by the NAACP, which condemned segregation, the stubborn sentiment in the nation was for Negro advancement "within the pattern of segregation." Virtually all southern white people, vast numbers of whites outside the south, and too many Negroes in and out of the South insisted on segregation. The Negroes prattled (and still prattle) that we could do better by ourselves, that non-segregation talk was "stirring up trouble between the races."

Roy Wilkins, "The Watchtower," *Los Angeles Sentinel*, January 1, 1948, 5.

Well, along came the President's Committee on Universal Military Training and recommended in its report that if young men were drafted, there should be no segregation.

Along came the lawyers for the NAACP and argued in the courts of Texas that segregated education per se was discriminatory and violative of the 14th Amendment to the Constitution. For the first time in legal history, evidence was placed in a court record on this point.

Then came the explosive report of the President's Committee on Civil Rights.[1] It said segregation must be abolished and that the time "is now." Quite a contrast to the slogan "the time is not ripe."

Before the end of the year, another Presidential Committee on Higher Education had made its report and it called for no segregation in schools.

In between this, Archbishop Ritter in St. Louis ordered all segregation abolished in the Catholic schools in that city. The Methodist women have condemned the segregated conference which contains all the Negroes in the Methodist church, and asked that it be abolished.

Not to be outdone by Presidential committees, priests, lawyers, and churchwomen, the world of sports did its bit. Jackie Robinson helped his team win the pennant and played in the World Series, the first Negro in that classic in the history of baseball. A Texas university—Southern Methodist—and Cotton Bowl officials invited Penn State, with its two Negro players, to the Cotton Bowl football game January 1.

We don't have all we want or need, but things are going our way. If 1948 is half as productive, we will be way up the road in 1949.

---

[1] See Document 31.

28

HENRY BROWN

Jackie, Campanella Break Texas Park Records

Chicago Defender, *April 17, 1948*

Regardless of the assault on Jim Crow, segregation proved to have great staying power. Even in baseball, while Robinson and other black players, such as Dodgers catcher Roy Campanella, could play with whites, black fans found barriers at the parks, as the case reported here from Fort Worth, Texas, shows. Henry Brown was a journalist for Chicago's major black newspaper, the Chicago Defender *(see Document 11).*

Fort Worth, Texas.—Jackie Robinson and Roy Campanella made baseball history in the Lone Star state on Saturday and Sunday, April 3 and 4. The two Negro players of the Brooklyn Dodgers were the first of their race to play against and with a professional baseball team in Texas.

Jackie played the entire nine innings of both games at first base and led off in the batting. Campanella caught the seventh, eighth, and ninth of both games.

The Fort Worth Cats of the Texas League is a farm club of the Brooklyn Dodgers. The Dodgers whipped the Cats, with Campanella scoring an important run in the ninth, 5–3 on Saturday, and came back Sunday to turn the Texas team back, 4–3, before 15,507 paid admissions, the largest crowd in Fort Worth's history.

Negro Fans Jim Crowed

Negro baseball fans, several thousand, were forced to stand behind the rope back of the foul [lines] in left and right field beyond third and first base, on Sunday.

Another 500 sat on the giant levee outside of the left-field wall. This levee is a barrier between the park and the Trinity River when the river goes on a rampage. To sit there, these Negro fans were charged the regular bleacher price of 90 cents each. . . .

From Henry Brown, "Jackie, Campanella Break Texas Park Records," *Chicago Defender,* April 17, 1948, 11.

... Johnny Van Cuyk walked to start the seventh [and] Robinson beat out a bunt ... [that] the third sacker [third baseman] couldn't field in time. This feat was a signal for the Negro fans, Jim Crowed along the first and third base foul lines and beyond the wall on the levee, to burst out with prolonged cheers. . . .

Saturday, the Dodgers played before the largest crowd of the spring training tour. There were 7,563 paid customers at the park.

29

CHICAGO DEFENDER

Reject Bowl Invite over Race Issue

December 4, 1948

Even though northern collegiate football allowed black players on some teams by 1948, local and state Jim Crow regulations still restricted integration in the South. This article from the widely distributed Chicago Defender *(see Document 11) shows how entrenched the color barrier remained in American sports and society.*

Easton, Pa.—Lafayette College here has rejected a bid to play Texas College of Mines in the Sun Bowl at El Paso, New Year's Day, because officials say the Texas school claimed Dave Showell, a Negro from Prospect Park, Pa., could not play.

Officials of Texas Mines deny saying they could not play against Showell, however. They claim all they did was to point out that he would have to stay in separate quarters from the rest of the team.

The situations came to a head when 1,500 demonstrators on the Lafayette campus demanded that the game be cancelled. Texas Mines officials insist they would be happy to have Showell get in the game.

Texas law forbids mixed competition, but in the last two years, Compton [California] Junior College has played in the state against a white school with a Negro on its [Compton's] team. Jackie Robinson has

---

played there against whites,[1] and Wally Triplett and Dennie Hoggard[2] played against Southern Methodist in the Cotton Bowl.

Members of the Lafayette team had voted to accept the bid before the racial angle came up. Dr. Ralphie C. Hutchinson, president of the school, announced that Athletic Director William Anderson rejected it following a telephone conversation with C. D. Belding of the Sun Bowl Association.

The bid may be renewed if other schools contacted do not accept it.

---

[1] Robinson played while stationed at Fort Hood, Texas, during World War II.

[2] In 1945, Triplett and Hoggard became the first two African Americans to play for Pennsylvania State University. Three years later, in 1948, they were the first blacks to play in the Cotton Bowl postseason game, which ended in a 13–13 tie with Southern Methodist University. In 1949, Triplett became the first African American player drafted into the National Football League.

30

BUDDY JOHNSON AND COUNT BASIE

Did You See Jackie Robinson Hit That Ball?

June 1949

The Library of Congress Copyright Office received several requests for song rights after Robinson debuted with the Dodgers, including songs with titles such as "The Jackie Robinson Boogie" and "Jackie Robinson Blues." The best-known song honoring Robinson was Buddy Johnson's "Did You See Jackie Robinson Hit That Ball?," which was recorded in June 1949 on the Decca label. The most famous version appeared on Victor records about the same time. The legendary jazz bandleader Count Basie rerecorded it, featuring vocalist Marion Joseph "Taps" Miller. The song peaked at number 13 on the music charts.

Buddy Johnson, "Did You See Jackie Robinson Hit That Ball?" June 1949, Library of Congress, Music Division, EU 169446.

Did you see Jackie Robinson hit that ball?
It went zoomin cross the left field wall.
Yeah, boy, yes, yes. Jackie hit that ball.

And when he swung his bat,
the crowd went wild,
because he knocked that ball a solid mile.
Yeah boy, yes, yes. Jackie hit that ball.

Satchel Paige[1] is mellow,
So is Campanella.
Newcombe and Doby, too.
But it's a natural fact,
when Jackie comes to bat,
the other team is through.

Did you see Jackie Robinson hit that ball?
Did he hit it? Yeah, and that ain't all.
He stole home.
Yes, yes, Jackie's real gone.

Did you see Jackie Robinson hit that ball?
Did he hit it? Yeah, and that ain't all.
He stole home.
Yes, yes, Jackie's real gone.
Jackie's a real gone guy.

---

[1] Satchell Paige was the great black pitcher who signed with the Cleveland Indians in 1948, catcher Roy Campanella and pitcher Don Newcombe were Robinson's African American Dodger teammates, and Larry Doby was the first black player in the American League, signing in July 1947 with the Cleveland Indians.

4

Cold War Civil Rights

31

HARRY S. TRUMAN

Special Message to Congress on Civil Rights

February 2, 1948

Risking reelection by confronting racism in his own Democratic party, President Harry S. Truman delivered on February 2, 1948, this historic message to Congress, the first federal endorsement of a civil rights plan since Reconstruction. Still, Truman took up the issue of civil rights later than other politicians, due to political calculations that on occasion had him backing away from support. This special message to both houses of Congress implemented the recommendations of the President's Committee on Civil Rights, which he had established by executive order in December 1946, and preceded two executive orders, issued in July 1948, that desegregated the civil service and the armed forces.

To the Congress of the United States: . . .

This Nation was founded by men and women who sought these shores that they might enjoy greater freedom and greater opportunity than they had known before. The founders of the United States proclaimed to the world the American belief that all men are created equal, and that governments are instituted to secure the inalienable rights with which all men are endowed. In the Declaration of Independence and the

From Harry S. Truman, "Special Message to Congress on Civil Rights," February 2, 1948, in *Public Papers of the Presidents: Harry S. Truman, 1945–1953, January 1 to December 31, 1948* (Washington, D.C.: Government Printing Office, 1964), vol. 4, 121–26.

Constitution of the United States, they eloquently expressed the aspirations of all mankind for equality and freedom.

These ideals inspired the peoples of other lands, and their practical fulfillment made the United States the hope of the oppressed everywhere. Throughout our history men and women of all colors and creeds, of all races and religions, have come to this country to escape tyranny and discrimination. Millions strong, they have helped build this democratic Nation and have constantly reinforced our devotion to the great ideals of liberty and equality. With those who preceded them, they have helped to fashion and strengthen our American faith—a faith that can be simply stated:

We believe that all men are created equal and that they have the right to equal justice under law.

We believe that all men have the right to freedom of thought and of expression and the right to worship as they please.

We believe that all men are entitled to equal opportunities for jobs, for homes, for good health and for education.

We believe that all men should have a voice in their government and that government should protect, not usurp, the rights of the people.

These are the basic civil rights which are the source and the support of our democracy.

Today, the American people enjoy more freedom and opportunity than ever before. Never in our history has there been better reason to hope for the complete realization of the ideals of liberty and equality.

We shall not, however, finally achieve the ideals for which this Nation was founded so long as any American suffers discrimination as a result of his race, or religion, or color, or the land of origin of his forefathers.

Unfortunately, there still are examples—flagrant examples—of discrimination which are utterly contrary to our ideals. Not all groups of our population are free from the fear of violence. Not all groups are free to live and work where they please or to improve their conditions of life by their own efforts. Not all groups enjoy the full privileges of citizenship and participation in the government under which they live.

We cannot be satisfied until all our people have equal opportunities for jobs, for homes, for education, for health, and for political expression, and until all our people have equal protection under the law.

One year ago I appointed a committee of fifteen distinguished Americans and asked them to appraise the condition of our civil rights and to recommend appropriate action by Federal, state and local governments.

The committee's appraisal has resulted in a frank and revealing report. This report emphasizes that our basic human freedoms are better cared for and more vigilantly defended than ever before. But it also makes clear that there is a serious gap between our ideals and some of our practices. This gap must be closed. . . .

The Federal Government has a clear duty to see that Constitutional guarantees of individual liberties and of equal protection under the laws are not denied or abridged anywhere in our Union. That duty is shared by all three branches of the Government, but it can be fulfilled only if the Congress enacts modern, comprehensive civil rights laws, adequate to the needs of the day, and demonstrating our continuing faith in the free way of life.

I recommend, therefore, that the Congress enact legislation at this session directed toward the following specific objectives:

1. Establishing a permanent Commission on Civil Rights, a Joint Congressional Committee on Civil Rights, and a Civil Rights Division in the Department of Justice.

2. Strengthening existing civil rights statutes.

3. Providing Federal protection against lynching.

4. Protecting more adequately the right to vote.

5. Establishing a Fair Employment Practice Commission to prevent unfair discrimination in employment.

6. Prohibiting discrimination in interstate transportation facilities.

7. Providing home-rule and suffrage in Presidential elections for the residents of the District of Columbia.

8. Providing Statehood for Hawaii and Alaska and a greater measure of self-government for our island possessions.

9. Equalizing the opportunities for residents of the United States to become naturalized citizens.

10. Settling the evacuation claims of Japanese-Americans.

. . . The peoples of the world are faced with the choice of freedom or enslavement, a choice between a form of government which harnesses the state in the service of the individual and a form of government which chains the individual to the needs of the state.

. . .

We know that our democracy is not perfect. But we do know that it offers freer, happier life to our people than any totalitarian nation has ever offered.

If we wish to inspire the peoples of the world whose freedom is in jeopardy, if we wish to restore hope to those who have already lost their civil liberties, if we wish to fulfill the promise that is ours, we must correct the remaining imperfections in our practice of democracy. We know the way. We need only the will.

HARRY S. TRUMAN

32

JACKIE ROBINSON

Statement to House Un-American Activities Committee

July 19, 1949

Robinson testified before the House Un-American Activities Committee (HUAC) regarding the pro-Soviet remarks of Paul Robeson, with a carefully worded script that Lester Granger of the National Urban League (America's most conservative black organization at the time) helped him craft. Not wishing to criticize Robeson, who had spoken out for integration in baseball, Robinson had also sought the advice of Branch Rickey. The Dodgers president counseled Robinson that it was an honor to appear before Congress. That the New York Times, *the only U.S. newspaper at the time with a truly national reach, covered Robinson's 1949 appearance in detail on its front page showed both Robinson's and Robeson's prominence.*

By that time, the socialist Robeson had set aside his acting and singing career to speak for political and social change. He had been an all-American football player at Rutgers University, from which he graduated in 1919. While earning a law degree from Columbia University, he also played professionally in the National Football League, before abandoning the sport and embarking on his entertainment career. An international star who lived abroad (including in the Soviet Union) much of the time,

---

From "Text of Jackie Robinson's Statement to House Unit," *New York Times*, July 19, 1949, 1, 14.

Robeson's theatrical and cinematic performances had made him one of the most famous figures in the world. He joined and subsequently chaired the anticolonial Council on African Affairs, which after World War II was listed as a subversive organization by the U.S. attorney general's office because of its affiliations with leftist organizations. The council also linked imperialism abroad to racism in the United States. Robeson backed labor and civil rights movements in the late 1940s, including an antilynching campaign that President Truman at first refused to endorse, and he actively supported the leftist Progressive party in the 1948 election.

The HUAC hearings explored Robeson's Communist affiliations, but he refused to implicate himself while continuing to defend the Soviet Union. Following the HUAC investigation into Robeson's political activities (which also called other black leaders besides Robinson to testify), the FBI canceled many of Robeson's concerts. His placement on anti-Communist blacklists (leftists were refused employment or appearances in the entertainment business), followed by the revocation of his passport in 1950, sharply curtailed his effectiveness as a spokesman, as well as his income. The U.S. government harassed him into the 1970s, twenty years after the HUAC witch hunts were over.

When the House Committee on Un-American Activities invited me to appear here today and express myself on the subject of your present interest, I answered that I would be glad to do so, although it isn't exactly pleasant to get involved in a political dispute when my field of earning a living is as far removed from politics as anybody can possibly imagine.

I am sure you know that I am a professional ballplayer. Baseball has been called the great American sport because all Americans get their kicks out of the game some way or other, no matter what their political or social connections may be. So it's customary, and I suppose pretty sensible, for ballplayers to keep out of partisan politics or any other kind of arguments and contests that may split their supporting public.

Of course, it will be said, and it's certainly true, that the question of Communist activity in the United States isn't partisan politics. But it's also true that some of the policies of this committee have become political issues. And so, naturally, I've had a great many messages come to me by wire, phone, and letter, urging me not to show up at this hearing. And I ought to make it plain that not all of this urging came from Communist sympathizers. Of course, most of it did. But some came from people for whom I have a lot of respect and who are just as opposed to Communist methods as I am.

And so it isn't very pleasant for me to find myself in the middle of a public argument that has nothing to do with the standing of the Dodgers in the pennant race — or even the pay raise I am going to ask Mr. Branch Rickey for next year.

"A Sense of Responsibility"

So you'll naturally ask, why did I stick my neck out by agreeing to be present, and why did I stand by my agreement in spite of advice to the contrary. It isn't easy to find the answer, but I guess it boils down to a sense of responsibility.

I don't pretend to be any expert on communism or any other kind of political "ism." Going to college at UCLA, . . . helping to fight a war, with about ten million other fellows, trying to break into professional baseball and then trying to make good with the Dodgers, and trying to save some money for the time when my legs lose their spring — all this, together with my family life, has been enough to keep me busy without becoming an "expert" — except on base-stealing or something like that.

But you can put me down as an expert on being a colored American, with thirty years of experience at it. And just like any other colored person with sense enough to look around him and understand what he sees, I know that life in these United States can be mighty tough for people who are a little different from the majority — in their skin color, or the way they worship their God, or the way they spell their names.

I'm not fooled because I've had a chance open to very few Negro Americans. It's true that I've been the laboratory specimen in a great change in organized baseball. I'm proud that I've made good on my assignment to the point where other colored players will find it easier to enter the game and go to the top. But I'm very well aware that even this limited job isn't finished yet. There are only three major league clubs with only seven colored players signed up, out of close to four hundred major league players on sixteen clubs.

Says Progress Goes On

But a start has been made, and progress goes on, and Southern fans as well as Northern fans are showing that they like the way things are working. And as long as the fans approve, we're going to keep on making progress, until we go the rest of the way in wiping Jim Crow out of American sports. . . .

We're going to make progress in other American fields besides baseball if we can get rid of some of the misunderstanding and confusion that the public still suffers from. I know I have a great desire and I think that I have some responsibility for helping to clear up that confusion. As I see it, there has been a terrific lot of misunderstanding on this subject of communism among Negroes in this country, and it's bound to hurt my people's cause unless it's cleared up.

The white public should start toward real understanding by appreciating that every single Negro who is worth his salt is going to resent any kind of slurs and discrimination because of his race, and he's going to use every bit of intelligence, such as he has, to stop it. This has got absolutely nothing to do with what Communists may or may not be trying to do.

And white people must realize that the more a Negro hates communism because it opposes democracy, the more he is going to hate any other influence that kills off democracy in this country—and that goes for racial discrimination in the Army, and segregation on trains and buses, and job discrimination because of religious beliefs or color or place of birth.

"Not Fooling Anyone"

And one other thing the American public ought to understand, if we are to make progress in this matter, is the fact that because it is a Communist who denounces injustice in the courts, police brutality, and lynching, when it happens, doesn't change the truth of his charges. Just because Communists kick up a big fuss over racial discrimination when it suits their purposes, a lot of people try to pretend that the whole issue is a creation of Communist imagination.

But they are not fooling anyone with this kind of pretense, and talk about "Communists stirring up Negroes to protest" only makes present misunderstanding worse than ever. Negroes were stirred up long before there was a Communist party, and they'll stay stirred up long after the party has disappeared—unless Jim Crow has disappeared by then as well.

I've been asked to express my views on Paul Robeson's statement in Paris to the effect that American Negroes would refuse to fight in any war against Russia because we love Russia so much. I haven't any comment to make, except that the statement, if Mr. Robeson actually made it, sounds very silly to me. But he has a right to his personal views, and if he wants to sound silly when he expresses them in public, that's his business and not mine. He's still a famous ex-athlete and a great singer and actor.

I understand that there are some few Negroes who are members of the Communist party, and in event of war with Russia, they would probably act just as any other Communists would. So would members of other minority and majority groups.

There are some colored pacifists, and they'd act just like pacifists of any color. And most Negroes—and Italians and Irish and Jews and Swedes and Slavs and other Americans—would act just as all these groups did in the last war. They'd do their best to help their country stay out of war; if unsuccessful, they'd do their best to help their country win the war—against Russia, or any other enemy that threatened us.

Not as "Any Defense"

This isn't said as any defense of the Negro's loyalty, because any loyalty that needs defense can't amount to much in the long run. And no one has ever questioned my race's loyalty except a few people who don't amount to very much.

What I'm trying to get across is that the American public is off on the wrong foot when it begins to think of radicalism in terms of any special minority group. It is thinking of this sort that gets people scared because one Negro, speaking to a Communist group in Paris, threatens an organized boycott by fifteen million members of his race.

I can't speak for any fifteen million people any more than any other one person can, but I know that I've got too much invested for my wife and child and myself in the future of this country, and I and other Americans of many races and faiths have too much invested in our country's welfare, for any of us to throw it away because of a siren song sung in bass.[1]

I am a religious man. Therefore, I cherish America where I am free to worship as I please, a privilege which some countries do not give. And I suspect that nine hundred and ninety-nine out of almost any thousand colored Americans you meet will tell you the same thing.

But that doesn't mean that we're going to stop fighting race discrimination in this country until we've got it licked. It means that we're going to fight it all the harder because our stake in the future is so big. We can win our fight without the Communists and we don't want their help.

---

[1] A reference to Robeson's deep singing voice.

33

JACKIE ROBINSON

Letter to President Dwight D. Eisenhower

May 13, 1958

*Robinson had generally been pleased with President Dwight D. Eisenhow-
er's support for civil rights. But he chafed at Eisenhower's unwillingness
to go further to end racism, massive white resistance to the Supreme
Court's rulings on desegregation, and physical intimidation of blacks.
On May 12, 1958, the president addressed the Summit Meeting of Negro
Leaders in Washington, D.C., arguing that African Americans had to
exercise patience on civil rights. In attendance at the speech, Robinson
sent this letter the next day to protest that view. Eisenhower wrote back
three weeks later, defending his record and urging further progress in
integration.*

My dear Mr. President:
I was sitting in the audience at the Summit Meeting of Negro Leaders
yesterday when you said we must have patience. On hearing you say
this, I felt like standing up and saying, "Oh no! Not again."

I respectfully remind you, sir, that we have been the most patient of
all people. When you said we must have self-respect, I wondered how
we could have self-respect and remain patient considering the treatment
accorded us through the years.

17 million Negroes cannot do as you suggest and wait for the hearts
of men to change. We want to enjoy now the rights that we feel we are
entitled to as Americans. This we cannot do unless we pursue aggres-
sively goals which all other Americans achieved over 150 years ago.

As chief executive of our nation, I respectfully suggest that you unwit-
tingly crush the spirit of freedom in Negroes by constantly urging forbearance and give hope to those pro-segregation leaders like Governor

---

Jackie Robinson to Dwight D. Eisenhower, letter, May 13, 1958, folder 142-A, box 731,
Official File, Dwight D. Eisenhower Library, Abilene, Kans.

Faubus[1] who would take from us even those freedoms we now enjoy. Your own experience with Governor Faubus is proof enough that forbearance and not eventual integration is the goal the pro-segregation leaders seek.

In my view, an unequivocal statement, backed up by action such as you demonstrated you could take last fall in dealing with Governor Faubus if it became necessary, would let it be known that America is determined to provide—in the near future—for Negroes—the freedoms we are entitled to under the constitution.

Respectfully yours,

JACKIE ROBINSON

---

[1] Governor Orval Faubus of Arkansas, who resisted Supreme Court–ordered integration of Little Rock's Central High School in the fall of 1957.

34

JACKIE ROBINSON

Telegram to President John F. Kennedy

June 15, 1963

On June 12, 1963, a white man gunned down Mississippi NAACP leader Medgar Evers in front of his house in Jackson. This heartfelt telegram from Robinson to President John F. Kennedy, sent three days after the murder, mentions the need to protect Martin Luther King Jr. at Evers's funeral. It also applauds the civil rights announcement that Kennedy made the night of Evers's murder. Two all-white juries in the Evers case deadlocked twice in 1963, and the killer, Byron De La Beckwith, remained free until he was convicted of murder more than thirty years later, in 1994. After Kennedy himself was assassinated, his successor, Lyndon Johnson, pressed Congress to pass the civil rights legislation requested by the slain president. The Civil Rights Act of 1964 was the most important civil rights law since Reconstruction.

Jackie Robinson to John F. Kennedy, telegram, June 15, 1963, folder 14, box 5, Jackie Robinson Papers, Library of Congress, Washington, D.C.

It might seem fantastic to imagine that even in the state of Mississippi anyone would seek to do injury to a non-violent leader like Dr. Martin Luther King as he goes there this morning on a mission of sorrow. Yet it was fantastic but true that some depraved assassin gunned down another man of non-violence, the late Medgar Evers, whose funeral Dr. King and his associates will be attending today in Jackson. Should harm come to Dr. King to add to the misery which decent Americans of both races experienced with the murder of Mr. Evers, the restraint of many people all over this nation might burst its bonds and bring about a brutal bloody holocaust the like of which this country has not seen. I therefore implore you, in the spirit of your recent magnificent appeal for justice, to utilize every federal facility to protect a man sorely needed for this era. For to millions, Martin King symbolizes the bearing forward of the torch for freedom, so savagely wrested from the dying grip of Medgar Evers. America needs, and the world cannot afford to lose, him to the whims of murderous maniacs.

JACKIE ROBINSON

35

JACKIE ROBINSON

Letter to Malcolm X

November 27, 1963

The controversial Malcolm X, born Malcolm Little, was a minister and human rights activist who preached Black Power and separatism. Detractors and integrationists such as Jackie Robinson believed that he also advocated black supremacy, racism, and violence. Malcolm X broke with the Black Muslim Nation of Islam and its leader, Elijah Muhammad, in 1964, preferring to unite religion with political activism on behalf of African Americans, before being gunned down by Elijah's followers in 1965. Robinson wrote this letter in response to a diatribe by Malcolm X against the former ballplayer that appeared in the New York Amsterdam News *(see Document 8). Malcolm accused Robinson of appeasing the "White*

Jackie Robinson to Malcolm X, letter, November 27, 1963, folder 35, box 4, Jackie Robinson Papers, Library of Congress, Washington, D.C.

Bosses" who ran America and oppressed blacks. In his eyes, Robinson cozied up to Republican politicians such as Richard Nixon and Nelson Rockefeller, betrayed Paul Robeson by acting as the black mouthpiece for anti-Communists (Document 32), and accepted servitude to white men — specifically, Branch Rickey in baseball and later William Black, founder of the Chock full o'Nuts company, who hired the retired sports star as director of personnel. Malcolm X could not stomach that Robinson seemingly trusted whites, even though they had murdered Medgar Evers just months before (Document 34). The exchange between the two black leaders is also notable because it came within days of the Kennedy assassination on November 22, 1963, which sent civil rights advocates reeling.

Dear Malcolm X:
Frankly, your letter to me was and is one of the things I shall "cherish." An attack by you is a tribute and I am honored to be in Dr. Bunche's[1] league. At least you have me in a dignified class.

I am honored to know that my "White Boss," Mr. Rickey, has been able to use me. I am also honored that many "White Bosses" marched with us in Washington and that many "White Bosses" are working with our top leadership to help us achieve equality here in America.

I will not dignify your remarks about my appearance before the Un-American Activities Committee except to say that if called upon to defend my country today I would gladly do so. No one sends me anywhere, Malcolm, nor will I hide behind any coattail as you do when caught in one of your numerous outlandish statements when you then revert to your out by saying "the Honorable Elijah ——."

Personally, I reject your racist views; I reject your dream of a separate state. I believe many Americans will not allow the thing that Medgar Evers died for to perish simply because you hate White people. Too many of our young people are dying as did the four youngsters in Birmingham[2] to go off into a separate state so the Honorable Elijah

---

[1] A political scientist at Howard University and diplomat, Ralph Bunche served in the United Nations and became the first black person to receive the Nobel Peace Prize, in 1950, for mediating the Arab–Israeli conflict in the late 1940s. He was appointed UN undersecretary-general in 1968. Bunche also marched with Martin Luther King Jr. in the March on Washington in 1963 and in Selma, Alabama. Malcolm X had denounced him for attacking Muslim radicals like himself and called him a sellout to the black race.

[2] A reference to the September 15, 1963, bombing of the 16th Street Baptist Church in Birmingham, Alabama, which killed four black girls and injured an additional 22 people.

Muhammad can be President and Malcolm X his immediate successor. Too many young people are in jail today and millions of dollars invested in our fight for freedom to heed your advice. Whether you like this country or not is of no concern to me. We are not perfect by a long shot but I happen to like it and will do all I can to make it a country my children [will] live in and be proud of.

As for Governor Rockefeller,[3] I sincerely hope that he, too, will be able to "use me." I do not know where you went to school but if it was to one of the Negro colleges, I venture to say a Rockefeller had something to do with it. I don't apologize for my support of Mr. Nixon.[4] If conditions were the same today as they were in 1960, I would still support him. I do not do things to please you, Malcolm, and it is obvious that I do not do things to please others if it doesn't please me. I, therefore, want you to know that I fully intend to do all I can for Governor Rockefeller. I respect him, his leadership, and what his family has meant to us. Because I support him does not mean you should. Rest assured, I am not doing so to have you come aboard.

You say I have never shown my appreciation. I assume that is why the NAACP gave [me] its Spingarn medal,[5] and why Dr. King has continuously asked me to participate in the SCLC[6] activities. That's why Rev. Wyatt Walker[7] allowed me to head the Burned Church Fund drive[8] and that's why the NAACP branches all over the country invite me to speak.

Negroes are not fooled by your vicious ideas that Negroes are dying for freedom to please the White man. Negroes are fighting for freedom and reject your racist views because we feel our stake in America is much greater than it would be in [a] "separate but equal" little state of our own.

[3] Nelson Rockefeller, the moderate Republican governor of New York from 1959 to 1973 and also U.S. vice president from 1974 to 1977, who was a staunch advocate for civil rights for minorities and women. Because of such advocacy, Robinson and Rockefeller established close ties, and Robinson supported the governor's unsuccessful bid for the Republican presidential nomination in 1964.

[4] The Republican Richard Nixon, who ran unsuccessfully for president in 1960.

[5] Awarded annually for outstanding achievement by an African American. Winners have included author W. E. B. Du Bois, jurist Thurgood Marshall, activists Rosa Parks and Jesse Jackson, and entertainers Paul Robeson and Oprah Winfrey. Robinson was the 1956 recipient.

[6] Southern Christian Leadership Conference, founded and led by King and others.

[7] Executive director of the SCLC and King's chief of staff, a founder of the Congress of Racial Equality (CORE), and a cultural historian and theologian active at home and abroad in civil rights movements into the late 1980s.

[8] Martin Luther King Jr. asked Robinson to head an SCLC fund-raising drive to rebuild three churches in south Georgia that had been burned by segregationists.

I do not know why Dr. Bunche speaks as he does about you and the Muslims, but let me tell you that as far as I am concerned, you and the Muslims are entitled to your views, your religion, and whatever else you believe in. I just happen to think you are not spouting the things that could possibly interest masses of people.

Thank God we have our Dr. Bunches, Roy Wilkins[es], Dr. Martin Luther Kings, Whitney Youngs, A. Phillip Randolphs.[9] I am also grateful for our "White Bosses" like Mr. Rickey and William Black and the millions of other decent White Americans who are in the struggle. I hate to think of where we would be if we followed your leadership. It, to me, is a sick leadership and should rightfully be rejected by the great majority of Americans, both Black and White.

[9] Whitney M. Young Jr. converted the National Urban League from a passive to an aggressive defender of civil rights. Labor organizer A. Philip Randolph was a leader in the early civil rights movement.

36

JACKIE ROBINSON

Address to Rochester Jaycees Luncheon Forum

September 20, 1966

Jackie Robinson was a businessman as well as a civil rights activist, and this speech to the upstate New York chapter of the United States Junior Chamber (Jaycees), a civic organization engaged in leadership training and community service, reveals his deep regard for both capitalism and politics. Many black-run businesses were thriving, but Robinson and other African American leaders sought true economic as well as political and social integration, in which blacks and whites shared mainstream markets such as banking, insurance, and retail. While Malcolm X and other Black Power activists preferred a separatist, "Black Capitalist" approach, moderate integrationists such as Robinson sought cooperation with the

Jackie Robinson, Address to Rochester Jaycees Luncheon Forum, September 20, 1966, folder 5, box 12, Jackie Robinson Papers, Library of Congress, Washington, D.C.

*white business community. This view reflected the changing focus of the
civil rights movement itself, as legal segregation declined but economic
discrimination persisted—and, in fact, became the target of Martin
Luther King Jr.'s Poor People's Campaign to support the rights of the
economically disadvantaged. This document is one of dozens that attest
to Robinson's frequent visits to business and civic organizations from the
1950s to the early 1970s.*

I am honored to be given the opportunity to share a few thoughts with
you at the first meeting of your luncheon group. I think it is a fine idea
for men who work in daily association to come together with other
employers and employees and to consider seriously and soberly the
great social issues which confront us. It is obvious that many of you are
aware that the business community has a challenging responsibility to
care what kind of society we are developing.

You'll have to forgive me if I don't offer you the traditional luncheon
speaker joke. I am sure that it is important that we never lose our sense
of humor. But I'm the kind of person who cannot be happy being deceit-
ful. I have to say and do those things in which I believe. And to be
quite truthful with you, when I think about Granada, Mississippi[1] and
Washington, D.C., I don't find much to joke about. I find, instead, that, as
a nation and as a people, we are facing very serious problems.

Like many of you, I am a father. Somehow, even though we have witnessed many different kinds of brutality taking place in this country, I
really never did believe I would read newspaper accounts about a mob
[of] big brave men with clubs physically beating twelve and thirteen-
year-old school children. I think that when this can happen in a community, that community has sunk into the very lowest depths. And I must
feel that a nation can only be as strong as its weakest link.

---

[1] Robinson is referring to the well-publicized battle for voting rights that had begun
in June 1966 and lasted well into the spring of 1967 in Grenada, a remote, central
Mississippi town. Civil rights activist James Meredith (the first African American
admitted to the University of Mississippi in 1962) had marched through Grenada,
protected by white officials who also permitted black registrars to sign up a thousand
black voters. But when the marchers left, it turned out that few African Americans had
actually been entered into the rolls. Martin Luther King Jr. and the Southern Christian
Leadership Conference returned to protest the suffrage violations, as well as to oversee
the integration of the schools. The white response to their efforts often turned into mob
violence.

I didn't really come here to talk about politics. On the other hand, sometimes when I note how the politicians are running things, I wish we could turn the country over to young, enlightened, progressive, tough-minded and fair-minded business men.

Seriously, I believe there is a next frontier—both for the American Negro and for American industry. Protests and demonstrations on behalf of civil rights have been both meaningful and effective. However, it is my conviction that the Negro citizen must now move to gain a secure position on two fronts—the economic and political fronts. It is my conviction that the next frontier for American industry is acceptance of the fact that there is no segment of our society better equipped to help solve racial problems than American industry. We believe the time has now come for the American businessman to take a commanding role in the solving of our racial problems and to realize the real and practical rewards which can become his, if he does so.

When I refer to moral rewards, I mean quite simply that the business community has a responsibility—not only to the Negro—but to all American society. I do not subscribe to the belief that the white American in 1966 ought to feel deep guilt because of the method by which some of his ancestors treated some of mine. I do not believe in the theory that the sins of the fathers ought to be visited against the sons. I am aware that, in truth, the white man was not the only guilty party in the slave trade. I am aware that black men sold other black men into slavery on the coast of Ghana. So I am interested in evening up things—not in getting even. I am interested in assuming my rightful place in American society, in the American economy, and in the American political system and I don't want to step on anyone or push anyone out of the way to do it. However, it must be done. I prefer it be done through cooperation. This is the American way.

There's another thing I must say—which some of my friends tell me I shouldn't say—and that is that I believe both white and black people in America waste too much time worrying about liking each other or being liked. I'll be very honest with you. If you want to like me, that's fine. But I can survive if you don't like me. Just give me my due and respect as a human personality, concede to me equality of opportunity and I'll do the rest. Along the same lines, I am not interested in getting to be a member of your social set unless such a relationship comes about normally and naturally and with mutuality. I think this country would make swifter progress along the road to real freedom if the white man understood that the black man wants to be his brother and not his brother-in-law. To sum it up—liking and love aren't what we are talking about here.

We are talking about respect. We are talking about sharing of goals and interests. We are talking about the Negro and the businessman working together to make America the America she can be and ought to be.

I submit to you that it has been proven to us in recent times that this kind of partnership is possible. I remind you of those days of stress and strain in Birmingham, Alabama, when pictures of police dogs at the throats of Negro children were flashed around the world. After a long and bitter and bloody siege, there took place in Birmingham what Dr. Martin Luther King called "a coalition of conscience." This coalition resulted in an agreement which ended the racial troubles then plaguing the city. Who was responsible for this? It was not the local politicians. It was not the local civic leaders. It was not the city or state government. It was the business community—men of sound common sense, men of honor, men who did not fear to negotiate. When business steps in at a time of crisis, solutions may be quickly found.

Finding solutions in crisis is vital. Yet, how much better it would be, how much more pleasant, how much more admirable if members of the business community took long and bold strides to better race relations before crisis comes.

Why wait for boycott? Why wait for picketing? Why wait?

Why not make up your mind to analyze the Negro Revolution? It won't go away. But it doesn't have to be what many businessmen regard it as being. It doesn't have to be a threat to business. It can be a potential. I guess it's a cliché now that there is a lush 25 billion dollar Negro market. Cliché or not, it is a fact that this market is ripe and ready for exploitation of the highest caliber. I see as a ringing challenge the need for today's businessman to acquaint himself with this market, to get to know more about the Negro people either from the standpoint of hiring them or courting their patronage.

I believe the Negro is maturing and is getting ready to assume a responsible place in this society.

I believe the modern businessman can perform a great service—not simply to a race of people—but to a nation and a world which sorely need help.

37

PAN AFRICAN PRESS

Robinson Backs Defense of Black Group, But Mrs. Basie Defers

July 17, 1968

This article, reprinted by the FBI and placed in its file on Jackie Robinson, arose from a flurry of commentary around a Brooklyn court incident involving the police and a small group of Black Panthers. The Pan African Press, a voice for cultural and political unity among African descendants around the world, expressed sympathy for militant civil rights activists and their battles with the government. Because of its strident stance against the white establishment, the newspaper was on the FBI's watch list as a subversive organization. Robinson disliked the Black Power movement. He thought of these sometimes violent revolutionaries as irresponsible agitators who would provoke moderate whites to elect segregationists such as Alabama governor George Wallace. But he also understood the justification behind their powerful message of militant self-defense — that blacks needed full rights immediately, including protection from racist authorities.

New York — Jackie Robinson came to the "defense" of the Black Panthers while Mrs. Count Basie [wife of the famous jazz bandleader] said they were "offensive" last week here. Robinson said it was disgraceful that 300 off-duty city cops jumped and beat up 12 Black Panthers, noting that the odds were far from "sporting."

Robinson . . . admitted that he, too, could have become a Black Panther as a teenager.

The goals of the Black Panther Party are no different than those of major civil rights groups, said Robinson. "The Black Panthers seek self-determination, protection of the Black community, decent housing and employment, and express opposition to police abuse," he said.

From "Robinson Backs Defense of Black Group, But Mrs. Basie Defers," *Pan African Press*, July 17, 1968.

The former Brooklyn Dodger great, who came to New York to meet with the militant Black group which has been stirring up a headline-storm, criticized police who are "trigger-happy" and "white people in general" who have "their heads sticking way down in the sands.

"They think by keeping their heads in the sands," said Robbie [Robinson], "that things will pass over and that things will be alright as long as we don't rock the boat and as long as we don't do things that will upset.

"I say that white America has got to get its head out of the sand and understand that we are not going to continue to tolerate the kinds of things that have gone on in the past," he continued. "There has to be a willingness to sit down and develop a dialogue. They have to recognize that Black people aren't asking for people to give them anything. We want to develop pride and dignity in ourselves and we can't do it on relief. But we also know that we have families to feed and therefore we are going to get as much as we possibly can. . . . There are not enough people around who give a damn about what is going on as far as the Black man is concerned," he said.

38

JACKIE ROBINSON

Letter to President Lyndon B. Johnson

April 18, 1967

As a supporter of Martin Luther King Jr. and of President Lyndon B. Johnson's efforts for African American equality, Robinson was in a bind regarding Johnson's escalation of the Vietnam War. Like King, Robinson opposed U.S. involvement in Vietnam as a distraction from the War on Poverty and other efforts to bring equality for African Americans. King broke with Johnson — once the darling of liberals and activists — over the issue. Robinson did not approve of King's decision. In this letter to the president, he assures Johnson that not all African Americans support King's position.

Jackie Robinson to Lyndon B. Johnson, letter, April 18, 1967, folder HU 2, 2/4/67–5/31/67, box 4, White House Central Files, Lyndon B. Johnson Library, Austin, Tex.

Dear Mr. President:

First, let me thank you for pursuing a course towards Civil Rights that no President in our history has pursued. I am confident your dedication will not only continue, but will be accelerated dependent on the needs of all Americans.

While I am certain your faith has been shaken by demonstrations against the Viet Nam war, I hope the actions of any one individual does not make you feel as Vice President Humphrey does, that Dr. King's stand will hurt the Civil Rights movement. It would not be fair to the thousands of our Negro fighting men who are giving their lives because they believe, in most instances, that our Viet Nam stand is just. There are hundreds of thousands of us at home who are not certain why we are in the war. We feel, however, that you and your staff know what is best and we are willing to support your efforts for a[n] honorable solution to the war.

I do feel you must make it infinitely clear, that regardless of who demonstrates, that your position will not change toward the rights of all people; that you will continue to press for justice for all Americans and that a strong stand now will have great effect upon young Negro Americans who could resort to violence unless they are reassured. Recent riots in Tennessee and Cleveland, Ohio is warning enough. Your concern based on causes and not on whether it will hurt the Civil Rights effort, could have a wholesale effect on our youth.

I appreciate the difficult role any President has. I believe, also, yours is perhaps the most difficult any President has had. I hope God gives you the wisdom and strength to come through this crisis at home, and that an end to the war in Viet Nam is achieved very soon.

Again Sir, let me thank you for your domestic stand on Civil Rights. We need an even firmer stand as the issues become more personal and the gap between black and white Americans get[s] wider.

Sincerely yours,

JACKIE ROBINSON

39

JACKIE ROBINSON

Letter to Deputy Special Assistant to the President Roland L. Elliott

April 20, 1972

On March 21, 1972, Robinson wrote to President Richard M. Nixon, whom he had endorsed in the 1960 presidential election, to decry the administration's civil rights record, particularly its slowdown on the desegregation of America's public schools. Nixon did not respond, a silence that showed how far the two had drifted apart. Roland Elliott, special assistant to the president, replied instead, and in turn Robinson sent Elliott this letter.

Dear Mr. Elliott:

Thanks for your letter of the 14th. I am sorry the President does not understand my concern. Black America, it seems, comes up short as presidents study or give time to fashion standards that are designed to help all Americans, when in reality, it is a smoke screen.

Black America has asked so little, but if you can't see the anger that comes from rejection, you are treading a dangerous course. We older blacks, unfortunately, were willing to wait. Today's young blacks are ready to explode! We had better take some definitive action or I am afraid the consequences could be nation shattering.

I hope you will listen to the cries of the black youth. We cannot afford additional conflict.

Sincerely,
JACKIE ROBINSON

Jackie Robinson to Roland L. Elliott, letter, April 20, 1972, folder GEN, HU 2-1, box 12, White House Central Files, Richard M. Nixon Library, Yorba Linda, Calif.

40

JACKIE ROBINSON

I Never Had It Made

1973

In I Never Had It Made: An Autobiography *(1973), published the year after he died, Robinson divulged his frustrations over the course of civil rights. This is his full autobiography, as told to coauthor and freelance writer Alfred Duckett. In it, Duckett expanded on his 1965 study,* Break-through to the Big League, *to reflect on Robinson's entire life. Thus the autobiography covers much more time than the memoir Robinson coauthored with Wendell Smith in the late 1940s,* Jackie Robinson: My Own Story *(Documents 5 and 9). Duckett, who was in public relations, also collaborated with Martin Luther King Jr. on a book, newspaper columns, and speeches, including the "I Have a Dream" speech in 1963.*

I thought I had learned the worst there was to learn about racial hatred in America. The year 1949 taught me more. A black man, even after he has proven himself on and off the playing field, will still be denied his rights. I am not talking about the things that happened to me in order to portray myself as some kind of martyr. I am recording them because I want to warn the white world that young blacks today are not will-ing—nor should they be—to endure the humiliations I did. I suffered them because I hoped to provide a better future for my children and for young black people everywhere, and because I naively believed that my sacrifices might help a little to make America the kind of country it was supposed to be. People have asked me, "Jack, what's your beef? You've got it made." I'm grateful for all the breaks and honors and opportuni-ties I've had, but I always believe I won't have it made until the humblest black kid in the most remote backwoods of America has it made.

It is not terribly difficult for the black man as an individual to enter into the white man's world and be partially accepted. However, if that

From Jackie Robinson, *I Never Had It Made: An Autobiography*, as told to Alfred Duckett (New York: HarperCollins, 1973), 78–79.

individual black man is, in the eyes of the white world, an "uppity nigger," he is in for a very hard time indeed. I can just hear my liberal white friends and a lot of Negroes who haven't yet got the word that they are black, protesting such an observation.

The late Malcolm X had a very interesting comment on the "progress" of the Negro. I disagreed with Malcolm vigorously in many areas during his earlier days,[1] but I certainly agreed with him when he said, "Don't tell me about progress the black man has made. You don't stick a knife ten inches deep in my back, pull it out three or four, then tell me I'm making progress."

Malcolm, in a few well-chosen words, captured the essence of the way most blacks, I believe, think today. Virtually every time the black stands up like a man to make a protest or tell a truth as he sees it, white folks and some white-minded black folks try to hush or shame him by singing out that "You've come a long way" routine. They fail to say that we've still got a long way to go because of the unjust head start the founding fathers of this country had on us and the handicaps they bestowed on the red men they robbed and the blacks they abducted and enslaved.

Whites are expert game-players in their contests to maintain absolute power. One of their time-honored gimmicks is to point to individual blacks who have achieved recognition: "But look at Ralph Bunche.[2] Think about Lena Horne[3] or Marian Anderson.[4] Look at Jackie Robinson. They made it."

As one of those who has "made it," I would like to be thought of as an inspiration to our young. But I don't want them lied to.

---

[1] See Document 35.

[2] Ralph Bunche, an academic and diplomat, was the first person of color awarded the Nobel Peace Prize, in 1950, for his mediation in the Middle East.

[3] An award-winning singer, actress, and dancer, Lena Horne was a civil rights activist who was blacklisted during the 1950s for her political views.

[4] One of the most celebrated contralto singers in history and a cultural ambassador for the United States, Marian Anderson famously sang at the Lincoln Memorial in 1939 before seventy-five thousand people with the approval of President Franklin Roosevelt and his wife, Eleanor, after the Daughters of the American Revolution refused to let her perform in Constitution Hall because she was black.

5

Remembering Robinson

41

JESSE JACKSON

Eulogy for Jackie Robinson

October 27, 1972

On October 24, 1972, Jackie Robinson died of a heart attack in Stamford, Connecticut. He was fifty-three years old. Three days later, the thirty-one-year-old Reverend Jesse Jackson, director of PUSH (People United to Save Humanity), gave the eulogy at Riverside Church in New York City. Robinson was the first vice president of PUSH, which Jackson founded in 1971 to advocate for black self-help and civil rights. Jackson had run the Chicago branch of Operation Breadbasket, an affiliate of the Southern Christian Leadership Conference designed to improve African American economic conditions; he was present when Martin Luther King Jr. was assassinated in 1968; and in 1984 he would form the National Rainbow Coalition, which absorbed PUSH into a political group that sponsored his run for the presidency of the United States that year. Among the celebrities and political dignitaries at the funeral were New York City mayor John Lindsay, New York governor Nelson Rockefeller, Democratic vice presidential candidate Sargent Shriver, and Atlanta Braves slugger Hank Aaron, who would break Babe Ruth's career home run record in 1974. Robinson was buried at Cypress Hills Cemetery in Brooklyn, alongside his mother-in-law and son, just off the cemetery's Jackie Robinson Parkway. This document is from the Harlem-based New York Amsterdam News *(see Document 8), to this day a widely read black newspaper.*

From "Thousands Mourn Jackie Robinson," *New York Amsterdam News*, November 4, 1972, A1.

Today, we must balance the tears of sorrow with tears of joy. When Jackie took the field, something reminded us of our birthright to be free.

He didn't integrate baseball for himself. He infiltrated it for all of us. His body was a temple of God, but his mind found no peace in wickedness. His powerful arms lifted not only bats but barriers. So let us mix the bitter with the sweet.

Jackie was neither a puppet of God nor one of other men. Progress does not roll in on the wheels of inevitability. In order for an ideal to become a reality, there must be a person, a personality to translate it.

He had options. He didn't have to do what he did. History calls on all of us to do something, but we are not always at home. He said "yes" in 1947 when he wanted to say "no." He could not hold out for himself. He had to hold up for us.

And in saying "yes," Jackie became a co-partner of God. Like a doctor immunized by God from catching the diseases he fought, Jackie fought for Blacks to get hope and whites concern.

The universe is dependent on person and personality to transport deliverance. Jackie Robinson was a balm in Gilead in America, in Ebbets Field. Hebrews needed a Moses, Indians needed a Gandhi. Science needed a Louis Pasteur. . . . We needed a Jackie Robinson.

He said "yes" in 1947 and pride in the Black community [welled] up when he took the field. He reminded us of our birthright to be free. He created ripples of possibility which seven years later the Supreme Court decision[1] confirmed.

For a fleeting moment, America tried democracy and it worked. For a fleeting moment, America became one nation under God. This man turned the stumbling block into a stepping stone.

Like life-giving oxygen, Jackie infiltrated baseball for us; thought he could bring justice into business but quit because he found no peace in wickedness. He was an instrument of peace, marched in Birmingham, Alabama, and castigated the power structure.

He accepted the honor of [the] Baseball Hall of Fame and no higher monument can be named for him than by naming Blacks as managers. Anything else would be a form of idolatry.

Like the graves of those who had gone before, Jackie's would bear his birth date and his death date: 1919–1972. We can determine our

---

[1] *Brown v. Board of Education of Topeka, Kansas*, the 1954 decision that struck down the "separate but equal" doctrine to mandate the desegregation of public schools.

birth date. We seldom know our death date. But on that dash between those two dates is where we live.

And for everyone, there is a dash of possibility, to choose the high road or the low road; to make things better or to make things worse. On that dash, he snapped the barbed wire of prejudice. He brought the gift of new expectations on that dash.

His feet danced on the base-paths. But it was more than a game. Jackie began playing a chess game. It was the Black knight and he check-mated bigotry.

In his last dash, Jackie stole home and Jackie is safe. His enemies can rest assured of that.

No grave can hold this body down because it belongs to the ages: and all of us are better off because the man with that body, the man with that soul and mission, passed this way.

42

ROBERT H. MITCHELL

Letter to Rachel Robinson

November 7, 1972

This letter is among hundreds that reflect on the meaning Robinson had for all Americans, especially for children. The impact of his breaking the color barrier in baseball had been felt around the country, and his death conjured up memories of the historic nature of the accomplishment. Robert Mitchell was the assistant attorney general of Oklahoma.

Dear Mrs. Robinson:

I want to share with you my moments and feelings about Jackie Robinson. It can only seem a shame not to be able to reach one's idol personally but upon reflection, it is perhaps much the sadder that a man like

Robert H. Mitchell to Mrs. Jackie Robinson, letter, November 7, 1972, folder 12, box 16, Jackie Robinson Papers, Library of Congress, Washington, D.C.

Jackie never knew that he played such an important part in many young men's formative years. My story is such a case.

In the summer of 1950 a schoolteacher took his 11 year old son to see his first major league baseball game in St. Louis, Missouri. Not only was it his first game, but it was an opportunity to see the team he adored, the Brooklyn Dodgers, and the idol he worshipped, Jackie Robinson. It was easy to admire Jackie Robinson but perhaps a little unusual for a skinny white kid from Oklahoma to want to become the next Jackie Robinson, but it was just such a desire that I had during that time. Just to be able to see the Dodgers in person working out prior to the game was overwhelming but the events that followed became almost too much for an 11 year old's heart to stand. My father and I were seated along the first base line in the upper deck deep into the crowd and under the overhang. Roy Campanella hit a high foul in the first inning which my father reached out and grabbed and tossed into my lap. He reports my eyes were about the size of two baseballs.

After the game, my father allowed me to stand outside the locker room waiting for my idols to appear with the hope of obtaining an autograph. There was only one autograph I was seeking. I waited for perhaps 30 or 45 minutes for Jackie to appear and then heard a commotion down the ramp and outside the stadium. Somehow Jackie had slipped out of the dressing room and into an automobile which was surrounded by at least 100 black kids seeking a touch or an autograph or a word. I immediately ran down to the car and danced around the circle, leaping high in the air and holding my ball over my head, hoping against hope that I would attract his attention and obtain his autograph. It was at that moment that you, Mrs. Robinson, apparently spotted me waving frantically. Jackie at that time was sweating profusely and signing autographs as fast as he could in the back seat. I remember so clearly your touching his arm and pointing to me on the outside of the crowd. I was easy to see since I was the only white face within a hundred feet. After a whispered word from you which, of course, I could not discern, Jackie leaned out the window and asked the kids to part so that I could come down and give him my baseball. There, before my shocked eyes, I obtained the autograph of a legend. That ball still is prominently displayed in my house.

There are so many adjectives that could describe his contribution and worth, all of which I am sure you've heard over these past weeks. For me, he was an inspiration, at first as a child because of his athletic ability, but later as a maturing adult because he had the courage of his convictions. More importantly now, his story shall be an inspiration for my two children, who are five and two. For them, Jackie Robinson will be a lesson to teach them that it is not the color of a man's skin but the man who is important, and that the ultimate test of one's worth is the courage to accept responsibility and stand by your convictions. I shall miss him.

Sincerely,
ROBERT H. MITCHELL

43

ROY WILKINS

What Has Jackie Done?

Las Vegas Review-Journal, *November 15, 1972*

NAACP leader Roy Wilkins (see Document 27) was among the many commentators who reflected on Robinson's influence in the black community. Wilkins had come under criticism from Robinson, who believed that the NAACP had been somewhat bypassed by civil rights activists because of its timidity and conservative bent. Nonetheless, Wilkins appreciated Robinson's contributions. This article by the former journalist and editor was likely disseminated widely, as it appeared in the Las Vegas Review-Journal, *a newspaper far from the center of American political culture.*

The ceremonies and the accompanying thinking that led up to the burial of Jack Roosevelt Robinson exposed once more a weakness in the knowledge of Negro Americans about themselves.

The body was on view at a Harlem funeral parlor to allow residents to pay their respects to the man who in 1947 had broken the color barrier in major league baseball. . . .

One woman who entered the chapel said she came because she "had no idea" of the insults that Jackie Robinson had endured. She was outraged at the accounts of the cruel tricks that plagued Robinson in the early years. It is hard to imagine any American black woman who does

From Roy Wilkins, "What Has Jackie Done?" *Las Vegas Review-Journal*, November 15, 1972, 56.

not know of the racial insults that confront any pioneer in the constant racial battle. That is why it is the height of cruelty for black children to be asked to crack a color line or to be placed in the midst of a racial dispute. They not only lose school but they are force-fed hateful ideas of human relationships.

An opinion was offered that some black young people don't understand Robinson's pioneering with the Brooklyn Dodgers and their question "What has Jackie ever done?" was cited.

This attitude marks an unthinking segment of black youth which knows little about their race. Some of the people who are yelling the loudest about black history ought to be made to design and teach courses in the achievements (and failures, too) of Negro Americans. In order to develop pride, the race may need to know that black kings led black people in Africa in 1500 A.D. But it needs as badly to know the history of Negroes here in America.

High on the long list will be the name of Jackie Robinson, for this man, by his talent and by his courage as a man, opened up new fields to his race. Every black player in the major leagues, every family owes a debt to Jackie Robinson. It is likely that every black athlete in any sport, even those that were opening [to African Americans], owes a part of his career to Robinson.

Aside from the salaries earned and the families these salaries support, Robinson created a new climate of tolerance and opportunity both in the world of sports and outside it. No opponent of Robinson will ever forget him. None of the thousands of sports writers can pass over the blazing Robinson era. Fans of every color applauded him. As the esteem for his exciting playing escalated, so did the opportunities for members of his race, including those far from the diamond.

What has Robinson ever done? His feats for his race, just by playing the game like the champion he was, are great enough. But he did something for white Americans, too. He released those who had known all along that the color line was wrong. And the other white doubters or hostile ones he converted through his batting skill, his daring on the bases. His own people came great distances to see him play in any city they could reach. The whites came, also, at first hoping to see him and the Dodgers fail, but later to cheer him and his race.

Life is not as spectacular as baseball. Everyone cannot steal home or stab liners at second base, or hit a home run. But if black young people are inspired by Jackie Robinson's life, then the human race will make a leap forward. More cannot be asked of any man.

44

RABBI A. JAMES RUDIN

In Memory of Jackie Robinson

November 26, 1972

In this tribute, Rabbi A. James Rudin, assistant director of the Interreligious Affairs Department of the American Jewish Committee, based in New York City, references Robinson's multiple influences. Beyond baseball and civil rights, Robinson also became a crusader against drugs near the end of his life, spurred to action by the death in 1971 of his son Jackie Jr., who had become addicted to drugs while serving in Vietnam. Robinson had long been a symbol for Jews regarding antidiscrimination and civil rights activities (Document 25), and he was so honored throughout his life by Jewish (and Christian) groups for his role in breaking down cultural and social barriers.

The untimely death of Jackie Robinson robbed America of one of its leading fighters for human rights. For some, Jackie Robinson will always remain number forty-two of the old Brooklyn Dodgers, a magnificent competitor and the first black to play major league baseball, an authentic culture hero who dramatically reshaped American life. For others, Jackie Robinson will always remain the concerned citizen who fought the evils of drug addiction among the young. And for still others, Jackie Robinson will always remain a powerful advocate for racial liberation and religious freedom.

This commentator will always remember two of Jackie Robinson's last public acts with special appreciation. He was an honorary sponsor of the National Interreligious Consultation on Soviet Jewry held in Chicago in March 1972, and last September he participated in a Community Memorial Service in New York in memory of the [eleven] slain members of the Israeli Olympic team [killed by Palestinian terrorists at the Munich Games]. May his memory always be for a blessing!

From Rabbi A. James Rudin, "In Memory of Jackie Robinson," November 26, 1972, folder 12, box 16, Jackie Robinson Papers, Library of Congress, Washington, D.C.

45

SCHOLASTIC

Interview with Rachel Robinson

February 11, 1998

Robinson's wife of twenty-six years, Rachel Isum Robinson, attended UCLA, where she met Jackie in 1941. When he retired from baseball, she pursued a career in nursing, eventually becoming a faculty member at the Yale School of Nursing and then director of nursing of the Connecticut Mental Health Center. In 1973, a year after Robinson's death, she established the Jackie Robinson Foundation. During Black History Month in February 1998, the publishing house Scholastic, a leader since 1920 in the field of children's education, arranged for students to interview the baseball legend's widow. Rachel Robinson reflected on her personal life with Jackie, the discrimination he faced, and his impact on the civil rights movement.

When Jackie started playing for the Brooklyn Dodgers, did you travel with him? How were you accepted by the other wives, players, and people you met?
When Jack began with the Dodgers in 1947—by the way, I never called him Jackie. The name didn't have the intimacy that calling him by his given name had. Anyway, in those days, wives were not permitted to travel with the team. The teams were saving money, and the men had roommates. . . .

Initially, one or two wives attempted to make me feel more comfortable as we sat in a special section of the ballpark for wives. But I think that the tensions were as evident in the stands as they were on the field. I became particularly close to Joan Hodges, the wife of [first baseman] Gil Hodges, Betty Erskine, the wife of [pitcher] Carl Erskine, and Pee Wee Reese's wife, Dotty, as well as the wives of the black players—[catcher] Roy Campanella and [pitcher] Don Newcombe.

From "Interview with Rachel Robinson," February 11, 1998, Scholastic.com, http://www.scholastic.com/teachers/article/interview-rachel-robinson.

How difficult was it for Jackie to honor his agreement to be silent for two years and not respond to negative behavior?
Jack made a pact with Branch Rickey, the general manager of the Dodgers and a pioneer in his own right. He would not respond to provocation regardless of what it was, or how much it hurt.

He was physically and verbally abused, particularly when he was on the road, in certain cities. The taunts angered him, sometimes frightened him, but he turned away from them.

I think the lesson for us is: If you have an overriding goal, a big goal that you're trying to achieve, there are times when you must transcend the obstacles that are being put in your way. Rise above them. Jack wanted to integrate athletics. He could not afford to create an incident on the field that would interfere with reaching this goal.

There had been predictions (at the time) that if you integrated sports, there would be riots in the stands and on the field, and races could not play together. He had to demonstrate that this was incorrect. Jack did so at considerable personal sacrifice. He was a personality who would usually fight back in an instant if he sensed that he was being mistreated. But he knew that he had to turn the other cheek for a short period of time — two years. That was a very clear part of the pact. So, he could bide his time knowing that it would come to an end, and he could soon be himself. . . .

How did Jackie feel when other African Americans entered Major League Baseball?
Jack always said that being the first to break the color barrier was important. But it didn't prove anything in the long run if there was not a second. In other words, he wanted to see the door opened for minorities. So, he was thrilled when Roy Campanella became the second African American in the National League and [Cleveland Indians outfielder] Larry Doby became the first African American to play in the American League. It meant to us that real social change was occurring in that system.

What was the worst or scariest experience you faced while Jackie played major league baseball? What was the worst experience for your husband?
From time to time, we received hate mail. And because it was necessary for Jack to continue to perform, and because taking those messages seriously meant I would live in fear, we ignored the mail. Then, one day,

we received a letter stating that Jack would be shot from the stands in a particular city. That was scary. We turned the letter in to the team, and asked that some measures be taken to protect Jack. It was hard then to believe that one could be killed because of one's race.

And yet, we knew of lynchings in the South, and we knew that the potential for violence always existed in the North as well. . . .

What was it, in your opinion, that gave Jackie so much courage?
I believe that he derived his sense of himself—his life mission, and the courage to carry it out—from his mother, Mallie Robinson. She was an extraordinary woman—courageous, determined, extremely religious, and self-reliant. She had been a sharecropper in Georgia. Her husband left her with five small children. So, she packed them up and took them to California, all alone.

Mallie managed to purchase a home for the family from her salary as a domestic worker. And she created an environment that was filled with positive values, as well as love. She was THE major influence on Jack's life.

A lot of people admired Jackie. Who was Jackie's hero?
In the early 1940s, Joe Louis, boxing's world heavyweight champion, was our hero. We felt that he didn't just fight in a ring, but he was battling the world on our behalf. He was fighting for respect, opportunity, and our place in America.

Later on, Jack met Martin Luther King, Jr. in the 1950s and early 1960s, when the reverend began organizing for the civil rights movement in the South. What Jack admired most about Dr. King was his nonviolent protest, and his use of organization and strategies that drew on the human spirit, and his sense of being entitled to all that America promised.

Did you or your husband ever regret that he decided to play in what had been an all-white league? Did Jackie ever feel like quitting?
No, we never regretted the decision. There were times when he felt like quitting, but he never expressed to me any intention to quit. He fought back by performing with excellence, and—as many sports writers said—he would answer with his bat. . . .

What was Jackie Robinson really like? Did he have a good personality?

I'm glad you asked that question, because most people only know his public persona: the tough guy always battling, very consumed with the struggles in America. But the family knew a different person. We knew a man very capable of great love and commitment. I always felt especially fortunate to be loved by him and to experience his great tenderness.

Even his vulnerability was more evident at home. He tended to be quiet and had great routines. He cherished the opportunity to gather the family together for dinner. Jack never drank or smoked, and felt that one respected the household by not using profane language at home—though I understand from his teammates that he could manage the language very well in the locker room.

He had a very strong sense of responsibility. Even in the post-baseball period, he worked very hard to get into the civil rights movement, and to work on behalf of others. He had an interesting statement to make about what life meant to him, which the Jackie Robinson Foundation now uses. It was: that a life is not important, except in its impact on the lives of others. . . .

What do you think was Jackie's proudest moment? . . .

I think I would say there were many proud moments in his lifetime, beginning with the birth of his children. We had always wanted a family, had learned to cherish family life from our own childhood, and so each birth brought great joy.

In terms of his profession, being elected to the Baseball Hall of Fame in the first year of his eligibility was a high point for him. He had not expected this honor because he had challenged the baseball writers often, and had antagonized some. And they were the ones who had to vote for him for this honor. So, this was a great thrill. . . .

What advice do you have for children today to continue what Jackie started in civil rights?

. . . I think at any age, one can look around in your own setting and in your own family and find ways to contribute to social change. When you see attitudes that hurt others, or limit their opportunities, you can say to yourself: what is my part in this? Can I be a catalyst for change in my school, on my block, in my church, wherever I am? The question is: do I have a responsibility for others? I would say yes, because I passionately believe that we are linked as human beings. Our destinies are intertwined. And what is happening to me ultimately is having an impact on you. So, if someone is homeless, uneducated, without medical care, without support, I have to feel some responsibility for them, and do whatever I can think to do. We all need to stand up and be counted.

I appreciate your listening to me today. . . . And I count on you to take the place of those who have gone ahead of you.

A Chronology of Jackie Robinson and Race Issues in Baseball and America (1867–2007)

1867 Amateur National Association of Base Ball Players resolves to keep black and white players on separate teams.

First "Colored Championship" held in Brooklyn, New York.

1876 Professional National League forms with eight white teams.

1885 Cuban Giants, the first all-black professional team, established in Babylon, New York.

1887 Organized baseball bans black players.

The Negro Colored Baseball League forms but lasts just one year.

1888 Color line in organized baseball becomes permanent until 1946.

1896 *Plessy v. Ferguson* ruling by U.S. Supreme Court legalizes "separate but equal" racial doctrine.

1919 *January 31* Jack Roosevelt Robinson born in Cairo, Georgia.

1920 First version of the Negro National League established; lasts in various incarnations until 1948.

1923 Robinson's mother moves family of five children to Pasadena, California.

1927 First version of Negro American League established.

1934 Effa Manley, owner of the Newark Eagles of the Negro National League, successfully boycotts New York City department stores for discriminatory hiring practices.

1935 Robinson enrolls at John Muir Technical High School.

Washington Senators owner Clark Griffith signs Cuban Bobby Estalella, who "passes" as white.

1937 Robinson enrolls at Pasadena Junior College.

Second version of the Negro American League established; lasts until 1950.

1938   Black journalist Sam Lacy asks Senators owner Griffith about signing black players.

1939   Robinson transfers to UCLA, where he letters in four sports.

Manley sponsors "Anti-Lynching Day" at Ruppert Stadium in Newark, New Jersey.

1941   *Spring*   Robinson leaves UCLA and becomes assistant athletic director of the local branch of the National Youth Administration.

June   Pressured by A. Philip Randolph's threat of a march on Washington, Franklin Roosevelt issues the first presidential order since Reconstruction to prohibit discrimination in employment practices.

Fall   Robinson plays semiprofessional football in Honolulu.

December   Robinson returns to Los Angeles following the Japanese attack on Pearl Harbor, Hawaii.

1942   Robinson is drafted into the U.S. Army.

Black press and Communist *Daily Worker* begin to lobby for baseball integration.

1943   Robinson commissioned as a second lieutenant at Fort Riley, Kansas.

Two Pacific Coast League teams consider tryouts for black players, but both withdraw offer.

Professional golf imposes "Caucasians-only" rule that excludes blacks from playing in PGA tournaments.

1944   Publication of Gunnar Myrdal's *An American Dilemma: The Negro Problem and Modern Democracy.*

Winter   New York State legislature prohibits discrimination based on color in employment.

May   Both St. Louis ball clubs announce that black fans will no longer be restricted to the bleachers and pavilions at Sportsman's Park.

July–August   Robinson refuses to adhere to Jim Crow bus seating at Fort Hood, Texas, and is court-martialed.

November   Robinson is discharged from the U.S. Army and agrees to a contract with the Kansas City Monarchs in the Negro Leagues.

November–December   Commissioner of Baseball Kenesaw Mountain Landis, who resisted integration, dies and is replaced by southerner Albert Benjamin "Happy" Chandler.

1945 *April* Robinson debuts with the Monarchs.

August New York City mayor Fiorello La Guardia's Anti-Discrimination Committee issues report on racial segregation in baseball.

August 28 Branch Rickey and Clyde Sukeforth interview Robinson and sign him in private to play for the Montreal Royals, the Dodgers' Triple-A farm team.

October 23 Robinson signs the Montreal contract in public.

1946 *Winter* Robinson weds Rachel Isum after a three-year engagement.

Collegiate and professional football integrate.

March 17 Robinson becomes the first black player since Moses Fleetwood Walker in 1888 to take the field in a game (exhibition) with whites.

April 18 Robinson debuts in Jersey City as the first African American to play in an official game of organized baseball.

August Joint Major League Steering Committee reports on the "race question," among other issues.

September Robinson named Most Valuable Player of the International League.

President Harry Truman creates the Civil Rights section in the Department of Justice.

1947 *January* Major league baseball owners secretly vote 15–1 against integration.

February Dodgers' spring training camp opens in Cuba.

March Southerner Dixie Walker leads a group of teammates who refuse to play with Robinson, but Rickey and manager Leo Durocher quell the mutiny.

April 10 Dodgers announce purchasing Robinson's contract from the Montreal Royals.

April 15 Robinson makes his National League debut at Ebbets Field, breaking the color barrier in major league baseball.

April 22 Philadelphia Phillies manager Ben Chapman mercilessly heckles Robinson.

July 5 Outfielder Larry Doby of the Cleveland Indians breaks the color barrier in the American League.

September Dodgers win the National League pennant, and Robinson is named Rookie of the Year.

September–October Robinson becomes the first African American to appear in the World Series.

1948 Teammate Pee Wee Reese shows public support of Robinson in the face of racial taunts.

Negro League ace Satchel Paige signs a contract with the Cleveland Indians.

President Harry Truman issues executive orders calling for the integration of the military and the civil service.

1949 Robinson testifies against civil rights activist Paul Robeson before the House Un-American Activities Committee.

The song "Did You See Jackie Robinson Hit That Ball?" reaches number 13 on the music charts.

Robinson is named the National League's Most Valuable Player.

1954 In *Brown v. Board of Education*, the U.S. Supreme Court overturns *Plessy v. Ferguson* to declare segregation in public schools unconstitutional.

1955 Robinson plays on the Dodgers' World Series championship team.

1957 Robinson retires from baseball and joins Chock full o'Nuts as its first black vice president and director of personnel.

President Dwight Eisenhower signs the first civil rights act since Reconstruction.

1960 Robinson supports Republican presidential candidate Richard Nixon, but Democrat John F. Kennedy is elected president.

1962 Robinson inducted into the Baseball Hall of Fame.

1963 *August 28* March on Washington for Jobs and Freedom.

November 22 President Kennedy assassinated; Lyndon B. Johnson becomes president.

1964 Congress passes the Civil Rights Act of 1964.

1964–1968 Summer race riots in major cities.

1965 Robinson becomes the first African American television analyst on the *Major League Baseball Game of the Week*.

Congress passes the Voting Rights Act of 1965.

February 21 Malcolm X assassinated.

1965–1966 Congress passes many of Johnson's Great Society domestic programs.

1966 Robinson named special assistant for community affairs under New York governor Nelson Rockefeller.

1967 Robinson resigns from the NAACP board to protest the election of the aging Roy Wilkins as president.

1968 *April 4* Martin Luther King Jr. assassinated.

June 6 Robert F. Kennedy assassinated.

1970 Jackie Robinson Construction Company established to serve low-income families.

1972 *October 24* Robinson dies of a heart attack in Stamford, Connecticut, at the age of fifty-three.

1973 Rachel Robinson establishes the Jackie Robinson Foundation to provide scholarships and leadership training for underserved populations.

1987 Dodgers general manager Al Campanis fired after making racist remarks during a televised interview.

National and American League Rookie of the Year Awards renamed the Jackie Robinson Awards.

1997 Robinson's jersey number, 42, retired throughout major league baseball on the half-century anniversary of his debut.

2004 Major League Baseball proclaims April 15 as annual Jackie Robinson Day.

2007 *April 15* To honor the sixtieth anniversary of his debut, major league players wear number 42 on Jackie Robinson Day.

Questions for Consideration

1. How did major league baseball defend itself when it came to segregation? What reasons did the baseball establishment, including the *Sporting News* (Document 19), give for resisting integration?
2. After reading his comments at various stages of the "great experiment," do you think Jackie Robinson was the right man at the right time to integrate organized baseball? See Documents 3, 5, 9, 15, 17, and 24.
3. How was the integration of baseball related to the civil rights movement in which it was embedded? See Documents 31–40.
4. What reasons did the two major reports commissioned by New York City mayor Fiorello La Guardia and the commissioner of baseball (Documents 4 and 12) provide for pursuing the great experiment? What were the authors' qualifications and warnings?
5. How did World War II affect the integration of baseball? Did the cold war have a similar effect? See especially Documents 31–40.
6. What was the impact of baseball integration on the Negro Leagues? Why did Negro League owners argue that they were owed compensation as a result of integration? See Document 20.
7. In your opinion, did Jackie Robinson succeed in breaking the color line because of his play on the field or because supporters of civil rights viewed him as a symbol of the fight against discrimination, regardless of his abilities? Why?
8. What role did African American fans play in ensuring that the great experiment succeeded?
9. Why was James Mannix (Document 26), a white man, so moved by Robinson's exploits?
10. How did organized baseball and the black and mainstream press gauge the success of the great experiment? See especially Documents 18–30. How would you gauge this experiment?
11. What lessons from the process of integration in baseball and Jackie Robinson's experiences did the black press draw?

12. Was baseball an effective medium for curbing Jim Crow and promoting civil rights in America? Why or why not?

13. What role did government—at the local, state, and federal levels—play in baseball's integration story? See especially Documents 4, 9, 27, and 31.

14. How and why did Robinson's struggles and accomplishments resonate with Jewish people? See especially Documents 25 and 44.

15. Why was Jackie Robinson so important to other racial and ethnic minorities who sought equal rights?

Selected Bibliography

PRIMARY-SOURCE COLLECTIONS

Library of Congress. A variety of collections of Robinson correspondence, memorabilia, and other sources; see http://memory.loc.gov/ammem /collections/robinson/. The Library of Congress also has access to the Jackie Robinson Papers and some of Branch Rickey's correspondence; see www.loc.gov/today/pr/2001/01-169.html.

National Archives, "Beyond the Playing Field—Jackie Robinson, Civil Rights Advocate," www.archives.gov/education/lessons/jackie-robinson/.

National Baseball Hall of Fame, http://baseballhall.org/hof/robinson-jackie.

Negro Leagues Baseball Museum, Kansas City, Mo., www.nlbm.com/.

University of Massachusetts, Jackie Robinson Educational Archives, www .umass.edu/pubaffs/jackie/.

MID-TWENTIETH-CENTURY U.S. RACE RELATIONS

Duberman, Martin. *Paul Robeson: A Biography*. New York: New Press, 2005.

Dudziak, Mary L. *Cold War Civil Rights: Race and the Image of American Democracy*. Princeton, N.J.: Princeton University Press, 2011.

Finkle, Lee. *Forum for Protest: The Black Press during World War II*. Rutherford, N.J.: Fairleigh Dickinson University Press, 1975.

Lawson, Steven F., and Charles Payne. *Debating the Civil Rights Movement, 1945–1968*. Lanham, Md.: Rowman & Littlefield, 2006.

Lieberman, Robbie, and Clarence Lang, eds. *Anticommunism and the African American Freedom Movement: "Another Side of the Story."* New York: Palgrave Macmillan, 2009.

Marable, Manning. *Race, Reform, and Rebellion: The Second Reconstruction and Beyond in Black America, 1945–2006*. 3rd ed. Oxford: University of Mississippi Press, 2007.

Myrdal, Gunnar. *An American Dilemma: The Negro Problem and Modern Democracy*. New York: Harper, 1944.

Smith, Ronald A. "The Paul Robeson–Jackie Robinson Saga and a Political Collision." *Journal of Sport History* 6, no. 2 (Summer 1979): 5–27.

RACE, ETHNICITY, AND SPORTS

Alpert, Rebecca T. *Out of Left Field: Jews and Black Baseball.* New York: Oxford University Press, 2011.

Bass, Amy. *In the Game: Race, Identity, and Sports in the Twentieth Century.* Houndsmill, UK: Palgrave Macmillan, 2005.

Burgos, Adrian. *Playing America's Game: Baseball, Latinos, and the Color Line.* Berkeley: University of California Press, 2007.

Early, Gerald. *A Level Playing Field: African American Athletes and the Republic of Sports.* Cambridge, Mass.: Harvard University Press, 2011.

Fetter, Henry D. "From 'Stooge' to 'Czar': Judge Landis, the *Daily Worker* and the Integration of Baseball." *American Communist History* 6, no. 1 (2007): 29–63.

Hoberman, John. *Darwin's Athletes: How Sport Has Damaged Black America and Preserved the Myth of Race.* Boston: Houghton Mifflin, 1997.

Klein, Alan M. *Baseball on the Border: The Tale of Two Laredos.* Princeton, N.J.: Princeton University Press, 1997.

Kurlansky, Mark. *Hank Greenberg: The Hero Who Didn't Want to Be One.* New Haven, Conn.: Yale University Press, 2011.

Martin, Charles. *Benching Jim Crow: The Rise and Fall of the Color Line in Southern College Sports, 1890–1980.* Champaign: University of Illinois Press, 2010.

Miller, Patrick B., and David K. Wiggins, eds. *Sport and the Color Line: Black Athletes and Race Relations in Twentieth-Century America.* New York: Routledge, 2004.

Powell, Shaun. *Souled Out? How Blacks Are Winning and Losing in Sports.* Champaign, Ill.: Human Kenetics, 2007.

Regalado, Samuel O. *Viva Baseball! Latin Major Leaguers and Their Special Hunger.* Champaign: University of Illinois Press, 2008.

Rhoden, William C. *Forty Million Dollar Slaves: The Rise, Fall, and Redemption of the Black Athlete.* New York: Crown, 2006.

Ross, Charles K. *Outside the Lines: African Americans and the Integration of the National Football League.* New York: NYU Press, 2001.

———, ed. *Race and Sport: The Struggle for Equality on and off the Field.* Oxford: University of Mississippi Press, 2006.

Ruck, Rob. *Raceball: How the Major Leagues Colonized the Black and Latin Game.* Boston: Beacon Press, 2011

Rust, Art, Jr. *"Get That Nigger Off the Field!": A Sparkling, Informal History of the Black Man in Baseball.* New York: Delacorte Press, 1976.

Silber, Irwin. *Press Box Red: The Story of Lester Rodney, the Communist Who Helped Break the Color Line in American Sports.* Philadelphia: Temple University Press, 2003.

Sklaroff, Lauren Rebecca. *Black Culture and the New Deal: The Quest for Civil Rights in the Roosevelt Era.* Chapel Hill: University of North Carolina Press, 2009.

Thomas, Damion L. *Globetrotting: African American Athletes and Cold War Politics*. Urbana: University of Illinois Press, 2012.

Wiggins, David K., and Patrick B. Miller. *The Unlevel Playing Field: A Documentary History of the African American Experience in Sport*. Champaign: University of Illinois Press, 2005.

Wise, Bill. *Louis Sockalexis: Native American Baseball Pioneer*. New York: Lee & Low, 2009.

AFRICAN AMERICAN BASEBALL BEFORE ROBINSON

Brashler, William. *Josh Gibson: A Life in the Negro Leagues*. Chicago: Ivan R. Dee, 2000.

Kirwin, Bill, ed. *Out of the Shadows: African American Baseball from the Cuban Giants to Jackie Robinson*. Lincoln: University of Nebraska Press, 2005.

Lamb, Chris. *Conspiracy of Silence: Sportswriters and the Long Campaign to Desegregate Baseball*. Lincoln: University of Nebraska Press, 2012.

Lanctot, Neil. *Negro League Baseball: The Rise and Ruin of a Black Institution*. Philadelphia: University of Pennsylvania Press, 2008.

Lomax, Michael E. *Black Baseball Entrepreneurs, 1860–1901: Operating by Any Means Necessary*. Syracuse, N.Y.: Syracuse University Press, 2003.

Luke, Bob. *The Most Famous Woman in Baseball: Effa Manley and the Negro Leagues*. Dulles, Va.: Potomac Books, 2011.

Peterson, Robert. *Only the Ball Was White: A History of Legendary Black Players and All-Black Professional Teams*. New York: Oxford University Press, 1970.

Rogosin, Donn. *Invisible Men: Life in Baseball's Negro Leagues*. Lincoln: University of Nebraska Press, 1983.

Zang, David W. *Fleet Walker's Divided Heart: The Life of Baseball's First Black Major Leaguer*. Lincoln: University of Nebraska Press, 1995.

JACKIE ROBINSON

Chalberg, John. *Rickey and Robinson: The Preacher, the Player, and America's Game*. Wheeling, Ill.: Harlan Davidson, 2000.

Dorinson, Joseph, and Joram Warmund, eds. *Jackie Robinson: Race, Sports, and the American Dream*. Armonk, N.Y.: M. E. Sharpe, 1998.

Eig, Jonathan. *Opening Day: The Story of Jackie Robinson's First Season*. New York: Simon & Schuster Paperbacks, 2007.

Falkner, David. *Great Time Coming: The Life of Jackie Robinson from Baseball to Birmingham*. New York: Touchstone, 1995.

Lowenfish, Lee. *Branch Rickey: Baseball's Ferocious Gentleman*. Lincoln: University of Nebraska Press, 2007.

Rampersad, Arnold. *Jackie Robinson: A Biography*. New York: Ballantine, 1997.

Robinson, Jackie. *First Class Citizenship: The Civil Rights Letters of Jackie Robinson.* Edited by Michael G. Long. New York: Times Books, 2007.

Robinson, Jackie, with Alfred Duckett,. *I Never Had It Made: Jackie Robinson, An Autobiography.* New York: HarperCollins, 1973; rept. 1995.

Robinson, Jackie, and Wendell Smith. *Jackie Robinson: My Own Story.* New York: Greenberg, 1948.

Robinson, Rachel. *Jackie Robinson: An Intimate Portrait.* New York: Harry N. Abrams, 1996.

Robinson, Sharon. *Stealing Home: An Intimate Family Portrait by the Daughter of Jackie Robinson.* New York: HarperCollins, 1996.

Stout, Glenn, and Dick Johnson. *Jackie Robinson: Between the Baselines.* San Francisco: Woodford Press, 1997.

Tygiel, Jules. *Baseball's Great Experiment: Jackie Robinson and His Legacy.* Exp. ed. New York: Oxford University Press, 1997.

———. "The Court-Martial of Jackie Robinson." *American Heritage,* July/ August 1984, 34–39.

———. *Extra Bases: Reflections on Jackie Robinson, Race, and Baseball History.* Lincoln: University of Nebraska Press, 2002.

———, ed. *The Jackie Robinson Reader: Perspectives on an American Hero.* New York: Plume, 1997.

Wilson, John R. M. *Jackie Robinson and the American Dilemma.* New York: Longman, 2010.

Acknowledgments (*continued from p. iv*)

Document 1. "A Fan Wants Negro Stars," *Daily Worker*, February 14, 1937, p. 14. Used by permission of Daily World Archives/PeoplesWorld.org. **Document 4.** September 28, 1945 report, from Mayor LaGuardia subject file correspondence (Box 3383, folder 12). Courtesy NYC Municipal Archives. **Document 5.** From Jackie Robinson and Wendell Smith, *Jackie Robinson: My Own Story* (New York: Greenberg, 1948), pp. 21–23. Used by permission of Rachel Robinson. **Document 6.** "Baseball Gives Contract to 1st Negro Player," *Chicago Daily Tribune*, October 25, 1945, p. 1. Used by permission of the Associated Press. **Document 7.** "Club Heads Give Views," *The New York Times*, October 24, 1945, p. 17. Used by permission of the Associated Press. **Document 8.** "A Crack in Baseball Jim Crow," *New York Amsterdam News*, November 3, 1945, p. 12. Used by permission of New York Amsterdam News. **Document 9.** From Jackie Robinson and Wendell Smith, *Jackie Robinson: My Own Story* (New York: Greenberg, 1948), pp. 80, 97–98. Used by permission of Rachel Robinson. **Document 10.** Wendell Smith, "It Was a Great Day in Jersey," *Pittsburgh Courier*, April 27, 1046, p. 26. Used by permission of the *New Pittsburgh Courier*. **Document 11.** "NAACP Youth Group Boycotts Dixie Club," *Chicago Defender*, May 25, 1946, p. 3. Reprinted with permission from Real Times, Inc. **Document 12.** From Joint Major League Steering Committee, Report to Commissioner of Baseball A.B. Chandler, August 27, 1946, pp. 18–20. © Major League Baseball. Major League Baseball trademarks and copyrights are used with permission of Major League Baseball Properties, Inc. **Document 13.** "Big Leaguers Put Okay on Robinson," *Pittsburgh Courier*, October 12, 1946, p. 26. Used by permission of the *New Pittsburgh Courier*. **Document 14.** "Adventures in Race Relations," *Chicago Defender*, November 2, 1946, p. 15. Reprinted with permission from Real Times, Inc. **Document 15.** "Jackie Robinson Says," *Pittsburgh Courier*, April 5, 1947, p. 14. Used by permission of the *New Pittsburgh Courier*. **Document 16.** "Royals' Star Signs with Brooks Today," *The New York Times*, April 11, 1947, © 1947 *The New York Times*. All rights reserved. Used by permission and protected by the Copyright Laws of the United States. The printing, copying, redistribution, or retransmission of the Content without express written permission is prohibited. **Document 17.** "Jackie Robinson Says," *Pittsburgh Courier*, April 19, 1947, p. 18. Used by permission of the *New Pittsburgh Courier*. **Document 18.** "Let's Help Jackie Do It!!!," *New York Amsterdam News*, April 19, 1947, p. 14. Used by permission of *New York Amsterdam News*. **Document 19.** "Editorial: A Negro in the Major Leagues," *Sporting News*, April 23, 1947, p. 12. Used by permission of Sporting News Magazine. **Document 20.** From Lester Rodney, "The Scoreboard," *Daily Worker*, April 29, 1947, p. 10. Used by permission of *Daily Worker* Archives/PeoplesWorld.org. **Document 22.** "Jackie Continues to 'Pack 'Em In' at Gate," *Atlanta Daily World*, May 27, 1947, p. 5. Reprinted with permission from Real Times, Inc. **Document 23.** © Bettmann/Corbis. **Document 24.** "Jackie Robinson Says," *Pittsburgh Courier*, May 17, 1947, p. 14. Used by permission of the *New Pittsburgh Courier*. **Document 25.** "The Meaning of Jackie for the Jewish Race," from *Jackie Robinson: Race, Sports, and the American Dream* by Joseph Dorinson and Joram Warmund. Reproduced with permission of M. E. Sharpe Incorporated via Copyright Clearance Center. **Document 26.** James A. Mannix, "An Open Letter to Jackie Robinson," Editorial, *New York Amsterdam News*, September 13, 1947, p. 16. Used by permission of *New York Amsterdam News*. **Document 28.** "Jackie, Campanella Break Texas Park Records," *Chicago Defender*, April 17, 1948, p. 11. Reprinted with permission from Real Times, Inc. **Document 29.** "Reject Bowl Invite over Race Issue," *Chicago Defender*, December 4, 1948, p. 13. Reprinted with permission from Real Times, Inc. **Document 30.** Buddy Johnson and Count Basie, "Did You See Jackie Robinson Hit That Ball?," June 1949, Library of Congress, Music Division, EU 169446. Reprinted by permission of Sophisticate Music Inc. **Document 32.** "Text of Jackie Robinson's Statement to House Unit," as published in the *New York Times*, July 19, 1949. Used with permission of The Associated Press. Copyright © 2013. All rights reserved. **Document 40.** From *I Never Had It Made: An Autobiography*, by Jackie Robinson, with Alfred Duckett, pp. 78–79. Used by permission of Rachel Robinson. **Document 41.** From "Thousands Mourn Jackie Robinson," *New York Amsterdam News*, November 4, 1972, p. A1. Used by permission of *New York Amsterdam News*. **Document 45.** Interview with Rachel Robinson, February 11, 1998. Used by permission of Rachel Robinson. **Figures 1 and 4.** Courtesy Hogan NBL. **Figures 2 and 3.** Courtesy National Baseball Hall of Fame Library, Cooperstown, N.Y.

154

Index